Why to Major in English if You're Not Going to Teach

Robert Prescott

Bradley University

Kendall Hunt
publishing company

Kendall Hunt
publishing company

www.kendallhunt.com
Send all inquiries to:
4050 Westmark Drive
Dubuque, IA 52004-1840

CONTENTS

FOREWORD:

The English Major and Industry

By

William D. Mayo
Retired Vice President, Caterpillar Inc.

For many years, English majors have graduated without a clear sense that their major has any relevance in the world of business. Increasingly, trends in globalization and technology have led English majors to feel like they are on the proverbial "outside" looking "in." Though eager to offer their liberal arts pedigrees in a challenging business environment, they seem even more unsure than their potential employers are about the value of their own college education. The business world seemingly belongs to the accountants, the finance majors, the computer geeks, the M.B.A.s, and, of course, the engineers. Conventional wisdom holds that English majors are better left to the teaching profession. But, as Thomas Jefferson once wrote, "Never fear the want of business. A man, who qualifies himself well for his calling, never fails of employment."

Let me be direct about this: those called to the humanities as a course of study, and specifically English majors, do indeed qualify for callings in business, and enlightened business leaders who hire these graduates will find them to be outstanding contributors to their enterprises. This is true not in spite of, but precisely because of their educational pursuits as English majors.

This book specifically highlights the many significant skills honed in the English major. Intuitively and immediately, one thinks of oral and written communication skills, but less obviously attendant in the English studies curriculum is the firm foundation laid for students to develop a more complex skills set: differentiated analytical skills; critical thinking and creative problem solving skills; research and computer technology skills; and perhaps most importantly, robust interpersonal skills that spring from an acute awareness of culture, literature, and writings of different peoples from around the world.

I recently retired from my elected position at Caterpillar, Inc., as Vice-President of North American Operations. I am not an engineer, nor am I an academician, accountant, finance major, or M.B.A. I am, quite simply, a businessman with 30 years of diverse experience in a global business enterprise. My academic credentials are also eclectic: a B.S in Oceanography from the United States Naval Academy, an Advanced Executive Education certificate from Dartmouth, and most recently my pursuit of a Masters degree in English studies at Bradley University. It is from my perspective as a global business leader, however, that I write on the issue of the relevance of English studies to industry.

Caterpillar, Inc, the world's leading manufacturer of earthmoving equipment and engines, headquartered in Peoria, Illinois, is not likely the first place one would look to find a large number of English or Liberal Arts majors gainfully employed. It is a global player with over 94,000 total employees and nearly 31,000 on the management payroll. Though the percentage of English majors employed is very small, I am aware of nearly 50 who are gainfully employed in important roles in the company.

Caterpillar is recognized as a world-renowned brand, and it is synonymous with quality. It is recognized as world-class in every sense of that phrase, and it is known to have not only the world's best construction equipment, but also the best distribution network. Over 180 Caterpillar dealers distribute Cat products in nearly every country around the globe. The capital these dealers employ in their business is two times that of the top four competitive dealer networks combined. It is this strength that allows Caterpillar's world-class brands to come along with world-class marketing, sales, and services.

One should know, however, that as oriented as this manufacturer and its dealers are to producing and marketing the best-designed, best-engineered, and best-supported products in the world, Caterpillar Group President Ed Rapp has said time and time again, "We are in the people business. We just happen to sell machines, engines, and parts." As important as engineers, accountants, finance majors, IT professionals, and M.B.A.s are in Caterpillar's business, their functional skills fundamentally empower a "people-to-people" business. With this in mind, the question of the relevance of English skills becomes moot.

Susan Connolly, Chief Operating Officer of Foley Machinery, a Caterpillar dealer in the Eastern United States shared the following assessment of business with me: "Business is nothing more than a collection of people trying to achieve a common goal. It is important that an individual be able to communicate with others to solve problems." Clearly, communication skills are not exclusively important to the English or Liberal Arts major. In fact, several years ago, while I headed up Caterpillar's dealer development function in Europe, I interviewed a number of high-ranking business leaders to determine their perspectives on this very issue, whether English studies are relevant to industry. Universally, the leaders I spoke with illuminated and confirmed Dr. Prescott's research that English majors can and do prosper and excel in the world of business.

To begin, I interviewed Mr. Lino Tedeschi, Chairman of Teknox Group (an association of seven Caterpillar dealerships in the Balkans). He holds degrees from the University of Turin, Harvard Law School, and has an M.B.A. from INSEAD, Fontainebleau. Lino leads a multinational business with nearly 1,000 employees in ten countries. When asked his perspectives on the relevance of an English degree to business, he offered this insight:

A great Russian poet once wrote that "literature is to life as must is to grapes." That's precisely why I do believe a degree in liberal arts is very relevant to business. But it must be achieved in a very competitive, first-class educational environment. Otherwise, you don't get enough "grapes," and they are not "pressed" enough. But if done well, the experience may be condensed to the point of making a genuine difference by bringing a better understanding of the world and of people, and above all, a creative approach to problem solving.

On the topic of differentiated skills attractive to business, I interviewed Chief Executive Officer Doug Whitehead of Finning International, a Caterpillar dealer in Canada, Chile, Argentina, and the United Kingdom. He had a great deal to say about "English skills" themselves:

> I think that the nature of studies in the liberal arts area, such as English studies, clearly expands one's mind in a number of areas . . . creativity, conceptual thinking, and out-of-the-box thinking. It also provides broader perspective, excellent written and verbal communication skills, and a desire to dig deeper to understand the broader causes of things rather than merely accepting things at face value. Often, there results a better understanding of people and greater empathy than linear-thinking engineers or business graduates can bring.

Mr. Robert Levy, Managing Director for CP Holdings, Caterpillar dealer in Israel and Hungary, offered a few new perspectives, dismissing stereotypical thought that would consider literature a "useless" pursuit and stressing the importance of intellectual character. Robert, by the way, holds degrees from Cambridge and is also an INSEAD M.B.A:

> I believe in the value of a university degree in that it forces a student to think and work in a disciplined way. I am not unduly interested in which subject matter is pursued. I believe leadership comes primarily from experience more than educational background. I have tried to avoid stereotypes of liberal arts students because I don't believe it to be fair. A good liberal arts student can go as far as he or she wishes in a business career. A poor one will not succeed. Personal traits such as intelligence, character, diligence, and honesty are more important.

Finally, retired Caterpillar Inc Marketing Manager, Francis Cuttat – who is Swiss-born, and a degreed Mechanical Engineer from Geneva Engineering School, adds this insight:

> People who are intellectually curious are people who want to progress and move forward with their thought process. To me, these are the kind of people I find stimulating and motivating. The world we live in is multidimensional. If it were compulsory to have a liberal arts degree in addition to an MBA, we would live in a better world.

On their own, these business leaders came naturally to the same conclusions showcased in this book. There is a *critical* place for the English major – indeed all liberal arts majors – in the realm of business. It is not now, nor was it ever, the "Would you like fries with that?" degree.

Speaking from personal experience, I have been fortunate to ascend to officer rank in a Fortune-50 company like Caterpillar. I have always subscribed to the adage, "Hire attitude – train skills." Indeed, with my bachelor's degree from the United States Naval Academy being in Oceanography, I brought little business acumen to my employer. Yet in nearly 30 years with Caterpillar, I served as a field service representative, a corporate accounts manager, a territory sales manager, a national sales director, general manager of a five billion dollar division, product development manager, and finally, as an elected officer of the company from 2005 to 2008.

I attribute that success, in every leadership position I've ever held from the United States Navy to Caterpillar, to my ability communicate—be that to communicate a vision, to communicate an example, or to communicate a sense of belonging to my team. That communication takes many forms—certainly the verbal form, but also visual cues, in the sense that people always observe their leaders for conflicting signals. And, of course, much communication takes the form of written discourse. Memos, emails, letters, policy directives – each of these communication "voices" says something to employees about the vision or purpose I stand for, the example or standards that I expect, and the community or family that unifies our organization around the common goals of the enterprise. In many vital ways, all business leadership comes down to discourse. Command of verbal and written communication skills is the fuel to any business endeavor. Simply stated, English Studies has helped me to become a more effective business leader within the human organization. And this reflects only the communication aspects of that discipline.

The diversified skills laid out in this book should hardly be trivialized. In today's global economy, more and more communication is written – designed to communicate across multiple time zones and cultures. The ability to translate complex ideas into clear understanding in a highly networked world is prized in business. Many times, teams are global – networked in real time via the Internet or web conferencing; often those team members may never meet face-to-face, with information moving at the speed of light. The ability to express oneself clearly marks people as leaders, and the inability to do so is a severe hindrance.

Robert Heinlein, renowned science fiction author and 1929 Annapolis graduate said, "One can lead a child to knowledge, but one cannot make him think." The comments made by the business leaders I've interviewed, coupled with my own 30 years of relevant industrial experience, suggest that English graduates do possess a distinct capacity for creative problem solving. To illustrate, the March, 2004 issue of *Property Week Magazine* article entitled "Cream of the Crop" states that "sharp witted English graduates are taking over from rosy-cheeked chaps studying estates management." This article reviews a growing trend among property management businesses to shun traditional property management specialist degrees in favor of what they term "non-cognate" recruits. There is an apparent growing preference for a "broader brain" over specialized property-management degreed candidates.

Likewise, in the *Corriere Della Sera* (Italy's leading newspaper), the esteemed Italian economist Francesco Giavazzi speaks of successfully competing in the global economy. He cites Win Bishoff, former CEO of Shroders, a British investment bank, stating that when he hires young people he followed "a precise rule":

first he runs through the list of graduates in classical literature, then mathematics; if he really cannot find anybody, he then hires a young person coming from the London School of Economics. Once hired, I invite them for lunch and I illustrate to them the problems of the bank. The graduates in classical literature and mathematics don't have a clue of what I am talking about; yet once in a while, their way of looking at things is so unusual, that all of a sudden, I understand how to solve a problem that up to that moment seemed unsolvable. As for the graduates of the London School of Economics, they repeat to me what I have read in *Business Week*. And I don't learn anything!

What Giavazzi and Bishoff suggest is that business, leadership and intellectual development are conjoined twins, joined at the head and dependent upon one another. Creativity and problem solving are sustained by a shared lifeblood of courageous thought – not merely by recitation and prescriptive process. These vital skills are nurtured not in the black-and-white world of functional educational regimen or tradition, but in the deliciously gray and provocatively blurry zones of evolving educational theory found in abundance within all liberal arts curricula, English especially.

To conclude, the English skills discussed in Dr. Prescott's book are indeed relevant. But what these skills are not also springs to mind. In my view, they are not just "nice to have," and they are certainly not simply the gateway to a teaching position. Indeed, the skills required for success in business today are firmly rooted in the liberal arts and English studies classrooms of the world's leading colleges and universities. Today's enlightened business leaders will avail themselves of the candidates emerging from these institutions and readily gather them in and mentor them into their businesses.

In industry, just as in government or politics, many times there are no lighted paths. But as the early 20th-century poet Antonio Machado tells us — "Travelers, there is no path. Paths are made by walking."

As a first piece of closing advice, I would echo Dr. Prescott's call to action for all English majors, that they be sure to apply their skills in internships and summer jobs in businesses and government agencies that excite them, so that when the time comes, they can confidently step out and confound the stereotypical view that they have no relevant or valuable skills. Without question, their skills are an outstanding foundation for success in business.

Second, I would speak directly to my fellow business leaders: hire liberally the best English majors you can find, and consider prying open the door of entry, even just a little bit. The individuals who step through that door, I'm sure, will surprise you, and your businesses will prosper because of them. Yes, indeed, English studies are relevant to business. Even in the macho world of heavy construction equipment and diesel engines. No, perhaps I should amend that. They are especially essential in Caterpillar's global business.

ACKNOWLEDGMENTS

Many people deserve my thanks for their contributions to this book. Prime among them is my wife Tracy, who has taught English at four colleges, two high schools, and one middle school for gifted children. In our many years together, her perspectives on the discipline of English have continually shaped my own.

I would also thank my colleagues in the Bradley English Department, who are devoted to all aspects of their English majors' success, in and out of the classroom. So, too, my colleagues in Bradley's Smith Career Center, who taught me how an English major's co-curricular experiences shape his or her early career path.

This book found its origin, however, through the inspiring guidance of David Black, now President of Eastern University in St. David's, Pennsylvania. It was he who first challenged me to articulate what I believed to be the relevance of English education to a student's professional future, and that subject has been my great passion now for twenty years.

Also instrumental in showing me all that can be done with a B.A. in English is my lifelong friend Jim Green, one of the most cultured attorneys in Washington D.C. I wish to thank as well my former student, Daniel Pfeiffer, whose assistance with my final manuscript was invaluable.

Finally, I would thank my friends at Kendall Hunt Publishing for providing the cover art for this book, which serves as a visual metaphor for the illumination of English Studies (the beautiful leather-bound volumes) that comes from the world of business (the banker's lamp).

INTRODUCTION:
Rethinking College English

Every year, thousands of young people, and some not so young, enroll as English majors at colleges and universities all across America. They come to the discipline for many reasons, but typically they choose English because they love to read or because they had a life-changing experience in a high-school or junior-college English class. Sometimes they come to English because they love to write creatively or because their verbal score on the ACT was in the 99th percentile and their math score was in the low 40s. What we almost never hear is that students chose the English major because their mom and dad told them to. Parents simply do not say to their kids, "No child of mine is going to major in Industrial Engineering. You are majoring in English or you're not going to college!"

Students never tell us that they are coming to English because they want to get a good paying job after they graduate. They do not stick with the discipline, in spite of poor performance, because they expect to waltz into a job afterwards. They come to English because they know they have a gift. They come because at some level, they know that they love to read and discuss literature, that they love to engage and critique the human experience in profoundly deep and moving ways. Our majors want to become better writers, better thinkers, better readers, and they trust that at the end of the process there will be a new path to follow, whether it be an entry-level job or another course of study at the graduate level.

Somehow, though, in the midst of all that healthy love of learning, they can begin to focus so exclusively on their writing and on their literary critique that they lose sight entirely of their need to do something with their degree when they graduate. When this happens, students find themselves at the end of a four-year degree process with no clear idea of what they want to do next or what, in fact, they *can* do next. This happens as often as it does because we who teach college English have not actively addressed the fact that the vast majority of our English majors do not go on to teach English. When we look out on a classroom, we are only seeing our students for who they are in the moment, not for the successful working people they will someday be, and thus we are not helping them see how their work with us is tied to their future careers.

Stanley Fish, one of the most well-known and influential English professors in the last forty years, issued an opinion on this issue in the January 6, 2008 *New York Times*. Fish rejects as "dishonest" any approach that recognizes the humanities as useful (English included):

> To the question "of what use are the humanities?", the only honest answer is none whatsoever. . . . An activity that cannot be justified is an activity that refuses to regard itself as instrumental to some larger good. The humanities are their own good. There is nothing more to say.

With similar ideas of noble impracticality in place, English curricula everywhere have been designed around the same academic model of English Studies that the faculty experienced in graduate school. In addition, the specific English courses offered at each school reflect the professors' individual specialties in research. The glaring disconnect here is that only a miniscule percentage of English majors goes on for the Ph.D., yet college English curricula are traditionally tailored to those students, with hardly any direct attention given to the futures of those English majors who do anything else but teach. Our "non-teaching" English majors therefore need to step back and rethink what they are doing with their experience of English Studies. So, too, do their professors, their parents, their academic and career counselors, and their employers.

I could not disagree with Stanley Fish more on this point. English *is* justifiable as a practical and useful academic major. It is justifiable as something in which both the government and private business should invest. But the "usefulness" of English, as most students experience it, is not to be found directly in the literature that the students and faculty discuss in class; it will not be found in the essays that students write and professors critique; nor will it be found in the literary criticism and theory through which students engage literature in new, highly disciplined ways. It is, however, to be found in a set of skills that rises out of all of those traditional activities outlined above. The usefulness of college English lies in a set of skills that English majors develop in ways unique to their discipline, skills that to the great surprise of many are among the most sought-after skills in countless areas of the working world.

English, as one of the traditional liberal-arts disciplines, has long been a successful means of preparation for a career in business, and it remains so today. Students will be much better served, however, if everyone involved in the English classroom understands that the most important objective of their shared work together is the development of a set of marketable skills. I say "marketable" here because in the world after college, a student's ability to think deeply, creatively, and critically about problems and challenges is needed in any professional circumstance; because the ability to communicate effectively with people with radical differences in culture and values is vitally important in most lines of work; and because the ability to adapt a message to the specific needs of a given audience and situation (the key element of successful writing) is not something that comes naturally to people, but rather is something that has to be developed over a lifetime.

English majors will be much more prepared to move on after graduation if their faculty and advisors help them see from the outset that their English *skills* themselves are their most important goal, not the discipline-specific means of building those skills. Today, students far too often approach graduation with no clear sense of what they are qualified to do as English graduates, no sense of what opportunities lie before them, and no clear understanding of the process that they need to go through to apply for their first entry-level job after college. And if their faculty cannot help them determine these things, how should they be expected to know on their own?

This book is designed to help fill that void in knowledge for everyone involved—student, teacher, advisor, parent—so that English majors can confidently approach employers and present themselves both in terms of their classroom education and in terms of the many ways that they used their English-major skills *outside* of the classroom. The first section examines in detail what English majors actually do for a living, what their skills are, and why those skills are important in the world of work. The second section looks at what we do in the English classroom to help students develop the English skill set. The book then closes with a series of chapters for prospective and current English majors to help them think about how they will apply for a job and move toward a long-term career path.

The college English classroom is constantly in flux, yet two important elements have always stayed the same: 1) a heavy dose of challenging reading that opens students' minds to the internal and external lives of human beings and 2) a heavy dose of analytical writing that interprets literature in a variety of different ways. My grandmother graduated from Carroll College in 1923 with a degree in "Literary Interpretation." She was one of a group of American women who examined literature from multiple points of view and who graduated from college as young intellectuals only three years after they gained the right to vote. Three years after that, a young man named B. F. Skinner would also graduate with his degree in English. In time, he would go on to found the branch of human psychology known today as Behaviorism. In 1930, Abe Fortas and Thurgood Marshall would graduate with their degrees in English—Fortas from Southwestern College and Marshall from Lincoln University—and in 1967 they would sit together as Associate Justices in the United States Supreme Court, the fifth Jewish and the first African-American members of the high court. In 1950, my friend Robert Thornton and his classmate William Peter Blatty both graduated with B.A. degrees from Georgetown University. Bob Thornton would later retire as Vice President and General Counsel of Caterpillar, Inc.; Blatty would complete his M.A. in English at Georgetown in 1954 and win the 1973 Academy Award for best adapted screenplay of his early novel *The Exorcist*. In every generation, in every type of English program, students leave college and begin career paths that take them places no one can predict at the time. What history does tell us, though, is that they will succeed in all areas of business and public service.

Today, America has almost 2,500 four-year colleges and universities, and at most of them, English is a very popular major. U.S. colleges graduated 55,000 English majors in 2006 alone, an average of almost twenty per school. At Knox College, for instance—where Lincoln argued the politics of slavery with Stephen Douglas in the fifth of their debates of 1858—English has been the most popular major in the college over the past ten years, with 367 students graduating with degrees in literature or creative writing. Not all programs will approach classroom practice in exactly the same way, but most will offer a blend of literature and composition, with an option for creative writing. Most will prefer a class size that allows for in-depth discussion. And very few, if any, will offer English education on a lecture model, as evidenced by the descriptions of department mission and practice available on every English Department's website.

Wherever students choose to go for their English education, they will work on their critical thinking skills, pitting their own interpretations against those of their classmates, their professors, and the critics whom they read. They will write a great deal, and they will have their writing challenged by their professors. And they will engage in hours and hours of oral in-class discussion in which they negotiate their alternative points of view with one another.

This book does not suggest that English classroom practice itself has to change, nor that English Ph.D. programs should stop advancing our understanding of the many ways in which we interpret literature. What change I *am* asking for, however, is that all the groups involved in college English—faculty, students, career advisors—work together much more openly and more often to prepare our non-teaching majors to make an easier and more successful transition from a degree in English to a satisfying and productive career after college.

SECTION I
WHY ENGLISH MAJORS BELONG IN BUSINESS

CHAPTER 1:
The English Major and the Job Market

Bradley University, where I have taught English since 1991, was founded by a visionary woman of the 19th century, Lydia Moss Bradley. When she started the university, her plan was that Bradley would "furnish its students with the means of living an independent, industrious and useful life by the aid of a practical knowledge of the useful arts and sciences." This book proceeds from the belief that the study of literature is one those arts that has a clear, practical use in society. I mean to show exactly why English majors are highly employable when they graduate from college and why they succeed so well in so many different types of work.

Parents naturally care about how their children's college degree programs will shape their futures, and so parents are often anxious about their son's or daughter's choice to major in—of all possible degree options—English. Many have no idea how the English major could possibly be a "practical" choice. Since 1988, I have taught and advised hundreds of English majors, and I have followed with great admiration the career paths of many of those graduates. The nature of my own students' careers, and the ways in which their career success is tied to their college major, is not unusual. Unfortunately, the success of English majors in their careers is scarcely understood. A great deal of research is routinely done each year to monitor the career paths of English majors, but somehow that information—vitally important to all those involved in college English—seldom reaches the students, their worried parents, or the employers who do the hiring. The news is good; the reporting of that news has been abysmal.

English Majors in the Workforce

The first thing for anyone involved with the English major to understand is that the vast majority of graduates in English work in some area of business or public service. In 2004, Neeta Fogg, Paul Harrington, and Thomas Harrington published the second edition of their book *College Majors Handbook*, which lays out statistical profiles of career information about graduates in sixty different majors. The U.S. Bureau of Labor Statistics provides the following key figures pertaining to undergraduate degree holders in English:

- 42% work in private, for-profit companies.
- Another 14% own their own businesses.
- 10% work for the government.
- 7% work in the non-profit sector.
- Only 27% work in education, and many of those people are not teachers.

In addition to those working, 20% of English graduates do not work. Three percent of degree holders are unemployed, and 17% choose not to work. Of that 17%, 7% are home with family, and 10% don't need to work (i.e. are financially "comfortable").

This means that 63% of employed English degree holders are working in business of some kind, with 10% more in government work. Yet English majors still are asked, "Do you plan to drive a taxi?" "Where are you going to teach?" or "Repeat after me, 'Would you like fries with that?'" For generations, English majors of all kinds have gone on to be leaders in all areas of the working world, and yet no one seems to have a credible, persuasive answer to the perennial question, "Why on earth would you major in English if you're not going to teach?"

The central purpose of this book is to answer that question, frankly and in detail. As unconvincing as it may sound on the surface, the simple answer to the question above is "Anything I set my mind to." English majors work in almost every area of business, and many of them succeed extraordinarily. A survey, for instance, done by ATT back in the 1970s found that a common undergraduate major among Fortune 500 CEOs was English, and that trend continues today. My own recent study of the Fortune 50 CEOs turned up the equally "impractical" discipline of History as one of the most common majors (the CEOs of Citigroup, Proctor & Gamble, Morgan Stanley, and Time Warner). Every person I have ever told about such survey findings has been absolutely shocked, and that shock speaks volumes about my colleagues' and my failure as English professors to communicate who, exactly, our students are and what it is that we do for them.

Traditionally, English professors have concerned themselves strictly with their individual research subjects and with their discipline-specific teaching. Because English is not directly related to any one career path, professors have typically been completely removed from their students' job-search process after graduation, unless those students were among the one percent who chose to go on for further study in English academe.

That lack of connection between a traditional model of English and the career needs of graduates has led us to this place where so few people genuinely see the relationship between Humanities education and the professions. An ivory-tower approach to teaching, in which the professor is not at all involved with a student's future outside the classroom, will still impart the skills an English major needs to succeed in business, but those skills will be an unintended windfall rather than the primary goal of both the students and their faculty. When little or nothing is done to help the student of English see the practicality of what transpires in the classroom, graduates can face tremendous uncertainty and anxiety once they complete their studies. Nonetheless, for generation after generation, students have majored in English and gone on to accomplish great things in all areas of the economy.

For those who might be prone to surprise at the idea that English is a very practical discipline, let me begin with one of the most shocking facts of all: English majors succeed in medicine, and they are increasingly sought after by medical school admissions boards. The September 10, 2007 issue of *Newsweek* ran an article titled, "Well-Rounded Docs: That's the goal as medical schools seek out and admit more non-science students. English majors welcome." One of the most stunning findings presented in the article is the fact that on the medical school admissions test (the MCAT), "Among the 2006 applicants to medical school, humanities majors outscored biology majors in all categories." The article quotes administrators at various levels of medical education emphasizing the importance of compassion, listening skills, and the ability to understand complex human issues outside the venue of the basic medical sciences.

This idea that humanistic education pays practical dividends is not new, of course, but it does seem to be a great secret that English majors who also show an aptitude for science can go on to vibrant careers in medicine. Dr. Harold E. Varmus, for instance, won the Nobel prize for medicine in 1989 for his groundbreaking research into the connection between human genetics and cancer. His undergraduate degree from Amherst College was in English, and he also studied 17th-Century Literature as a graduate student at Harvard University. Likewise, Lisa Toepp, M.D., (co-valedictorian of my high school graduating class) began her education with B.A. in English from the University of Illinois and is now a child, adolescent, and forensic psychiatrist for the State of Colorado, having retired from the United States Army as a full colonel. The Chief of Medical Staff at her hospital, Dr. Albert Singleton, M.D., received his B.A. in English at the University of Texas at Austin; and his daughter, Terrell Singleton, M.D., did her B.A. in English at the University of Colorado and is currently the chief resident in general surgery at the University of Texas Medical Branch in Galveston. On a more overtly literary note, the great American poet William Carlos Williams, European educated, chose a professional education in medicine as a means of supporting his ambitions as a writer. He went on to deliver over 3,000 babies and to win the Pulitzer Prize for poetry.

Dr. Toepp is happy to speak today about the importance of her English education to her success in medicine:

> My studies as an English major developed my muscles for thinking deeply, for synthesizing seemingly unrelated data and clues, and developing hypotheses. My skills in critical thinking, reading, writing, and oral communication, sharpened during my undergraduate years as an English major, have served me well in my career as a physician. By specializing in psychiatry, I continually satisfy my insatiable curiosity about the complexities of human nature.

She highlights not only the English major's skills in analysis and communication, she speaks to the English major's fascination with human nature itself, examined so deeply in the literature of all nations.

A background in English gives both clinical and research physicians training and experience listening to people very different from them speak to deeply emotional issues; it breeds both empathy and tolerance; it teaches them how to match a message to the needs of a particular audience, even if that audience is angry or suffering, even if the subject itself causes the audience pain. Successful communication is not about grammatical exactness, it is about meeting the needs of the audience at hand. No one, regardless of IQ, vocabulary, or advanced degrees accrued, can do that without understanding where the audience is coming from—culturally, intellectually, psychologically, spiritually. Our *best* physicians are not only good at the mechanics of their trade, they are humane—i.e. empathetic, respectful, emotionally aware—and they are good at "reading" their patients and communicating with them, no matter how different each patient is one to the next. The medical sciences do not teach those skills; English does.

Medicine, however, is by no means the only field in which English majors succeed to the great surprise of their co-workers. They also turn up in all areas of business, whether it be the life-insurance industry, corporate real estate, investment banking, public relations, marketing, or the mid- and upper-level management positions of almost all sectors of corporate America. A very well-known example would be Jill Barad, the former CEO of Mattel Corporation. The story of her meteoric rise in management made the front page of the *Wall Street Journal* and was the cover story for the May 25, 1998 issue of *Business Week*. Ms. Barad graduated from Queens College with a degree in English—as well as a tremendous amount of energy, imagination, and interpersonal skill. Between her junior and senior years, she took time out to sell makeup for Love Cosmetics, and she continued in that line of work after graduation in upstate New York as a "traveling cosmetician-trainer." While traveling from store to store, she noticed that Coty's displays were ineffective, and so she sent a report outlining a better wall display design, and the company wound up using her idea for the next 20 years.

After relocating to Los Angeles, Ms. Barad showed that same creativity and the same understanding of how to reach the public when she took a job with Mattel's novelty development unit. In an attempt to demonstrate her innovative marketing skills for Mattel, she produced a low-budget commercial for her own product—a childrens' toy called "A Bad Case of Worms." That imaginative and fairly audacious tape drew her to the attention of management, and though the rubber worms failed to sell, she had a great success with the first female action figure (She-Ra), and she was soon made a product manager for the Barbie line, the work that propelled her to the office of President and CEO. It was Jill Barad who revolutionized Barbie, re-establishing the doll's popularity with mothers and daughters whose sensibilities were no longer tied to the doll's 1960s origins.

Barad knew where her audience was coming from, and she helped Mattel send a message that hit home. One of the first successes was "Day to Night Barbie"—a hard-working corporate woman by day and a hard-partying single girl by night. It was a smash hit. Her brilliant business strategy was to "segment" what was one product into a series of products that children would play with in different ways, thus spurring multiple sales where before there would have been only one. The response to veterinarian Barbie, business-woman Barbie, and Harley Barbie was a change from $200 million in 1981 to $1.7 billion in 1996. After a controversial parting with Mattel, Ms. Barad is still often featured in the *Wall Street Journal* and in trade magazines of all kinds, and she is a highly sought-after speaker to present her ideas and experiences as someone who as a woman broke through the glass ceiling of upper-management.

Like Jill Barad, Andrea Jung also rose to prominence in the 1990s as the CEO of the Avon Corporation, a company right in the middle of the Fortune 500. Her undergraduate degree in English was from Princeton, and her career in retailing began with Bloomingdale's management trainee program. She then moved up the corporate ladder with I. Magnan and then with Nieman Marcus. In 1994 she moved again to Avon as the Chief Operations Officer in Global marketing and then became President and CEO of a cosmetics company with annual sales over $8,000,000,000 in over one hundred countries.

In the next decade, more women with undergraduate English degrees reached the level of CEO, one of the most celebrated being Anne Mulcahy (B.A. English from Marymount College, 1974), the CEO and Chairman of the Board of the Xerox Corporation. Her rise in business has also been covered by *Fortune*, *Time*, and *Business Week*. When she was promoted to CEO in 2000, after 24 years of service to the company, Xerox had a debt load of $17.1 billion and a cash reserve of $154 million. In the process of turning the company around, Mulcahy showed a gift for seeking out sound expert advice and for choosing team-mates with creative vision, three of the most important being Ursula Burns (the company's former head of manufacturing), North American Operations Chief Jim Firestone, and CFO Larry Zimmerman (formerly of IBM). Mulcahy is also described by many as being able to accept and to give harsh, blunt analyses of what has not been working in a business—always in the effort to find a solution. During the painful time of restructuring, this leadership team met bi-weekly for strategy sessions that *Fortune* reporter Betsy Morris praises for their "brutal honesty and vigorous debate." Mulcahy expects her team to come back to her with compromise positions if they have a better idea than the one she ordered.

By March of 2003, Xerox had reduced its debt by 21% and they now had $3 billion in cash, as opposed to the $154 million of three years earlier, and by 2007 the debt had been reduced to $7 billion (a 60% drop), and net earnings had increased to $1.2 billion. *Fortune* magazine ran an article in October of 2007 entitled "Dynamic Duo" to outline the historic success that Mulcahy and her team had put together for Xerox, and the article focuses primarily on the first situation in which a female CEO of a Fortune-500 company would turn over the reins of the company to another woman, in this case to Ursula Burns, and that in fact did happen in June of 2009.

Nationally, most college English majors are women, roughly sixty percent, but men also succeed in business with an English degree. In June of 2008, for instance, Aylwin B. Lewis took over as President and CEO of Potbelly Sandwich works, having served already as President and CEO of Sears Holding Corporation (2005-2008), and before that the K-Mart Holding Corporation, which in turn merged with Sears, Roebuck and Company after Lewis had been CEO of Kmart for only a year.

Lewis completed his B.A. in English at the University of Houston in 1976, and speaking to reporters Barbara Rose and Michael Oneal in a November 21, 2004 *Chicago Tribune* article, he shared that he was dissuaded from pursuing a career as a professor by discovering that he loved restaurant management from his college job at a local Houston Jack-in-the-Box franchise. Lewis explains in that article that he had intended to complete a Ph.D. in English, but that instead he "fell in love with the notion of serving customers" while he was working for Jack-in-the-Box to make ends meet.

With his strong interpersonal skills, ethical vision, and ability to communicate with customers and employees alike, Lewis embarked on a meteoric career, from his early beginning as a management trainee at a fast-food restaurant, he moved next to Yum Brands—a giant, multiple-restaurant company—and he rose through the corporate ranks of the KFC and Pizza Hut Divisions of Yum.

Then, in what many business minds thought a high-risk venture, Lewis took over Kmart in October of 2004 when Kmart's financial situation was far from firm, having to deal as they did with competitors as strong as Wal-Mart and Target. Nonetheless, in just over five months, K-mart merged with Sears, and Lewis found himself in charge of a company with nearly 4,000 stores and 55 billion dollars in annual revenue. How fitting, then, that the young English major who *loved* his job at Jack-in-the-Box has now returned to the restaurant business as one of the leading African-American business leaders in the world and as a member of the corporate boards of both Disney and Halliburton.

No one simply leaves an undergraduate program in English, however, and moves immediately into upper management anywhere. In all four of the cases outlined above, the companies' financial success rode in large measure on the CEO's ability to analyze problems, to think creatively, to communicate with a team of company leaders along a long, arduous road of hard work. Certainly, such a person also needs statistical skills and a keen analytical mind, but nothing is more important than the ability to understand the marketplace (made up entirely of human beings) and to communicate in that marketplace how the products and services of that company have something more to offer than those of their competitors. By training English majors how to understand diverse audiences, how to write to those audiences, and how to think critically and creatively, we in the discipline of English are preparing our students in ways that cannot be picked up "on the job."

In a 1996 interview on PBS's *NewsHour*, the former CEO of IBM, Leo Gerstner, spoke about the importance of working on English skills *before* coming into the workplace, having given a speech the day before as a part of the first National Education Summit, and his words speak to the crucial importance of the English skills set:

> We're not looking for the schools to teach vocational skills. I can teach engineers and other people who come to IBM how to work with machines, how to do marketing, how to do finance, but we're really not equipped to teach 'em to read and to write.

Excellence in reading and writing entails much more than anyone learns in high school, and indeed, once someone is working in a fast-paced, competitive marketplace, there is little time to work on one's critical-thinking skills, and there are no writing teachers who will give the painful, individualized feedback one needs in order to grow as a writer. English majors bring those skills to their very first positions, at the bottom of the long road to success in business, but those skills are vital to any such success.

The Apprenticeship Period

That path, that road to "success," is distinctly different for an English major from what it is for a Finance major or a Business-Management major. It is, from the outset, at least, much more uncertain, more undefined. This is why at large-university graduations, the business college graduates will chant "We've got jobs," "We've got jobs," while the English majors sit quietly and wonder how long they can stay surfing in Costa Rica before they have to come home and think about a future. They wonder how long their savings account will allow them to jump horses in Ecuador. They wonder if the Cannes Film Festival will still be going on by the time they get there. But underneath those thoughts, while the English majors listen to the chanting of their securely employed friends, they are, at some level, envious of that security, or they are at least annoyed because their parents and grandparents envy that security on their behalf.

That natural fear, that envy, that insecurity has never been necessary or realistic. What English majors and their concerned families need to understand and embrace is that an English major—like any humanities major—will enter into some kind of apprenticeship period after graduation, and that period of learning, whether it be in graduate school or in the workplace, will determine their future in ways that cannot be anticipated. Every English major who does not go into teaching will go through some three- to five-year process in which he or she acquires a specific set of skills—on the job, in a classroom setting, or in a combination of both—and at some point that combination of their English skills and their new skills will lead them forward in a way that neither skills set could do on its own. English majors need to expect that apprenticeship period, to look forward to it, and to choose what they will specialize in with forethought so that the work will bring them a deep, personal satisfaction. They can do that because they have an entire world of options from which to choose.

Money Matters: Analysis of Wages for English Majors

No examination of the English major and the job market could be complete without an objective look at salaries. Assuming that people can agree that money is not the sole measure of success, reasonable people should well ask what the financial outcome would be of a student's choice to pursue a career with an English major rather than a major in Business. For those who consider English an impractical choice of college major, the statistical facts regarding English graduates' wages provided again by the *College Majors Handbook* may help turn such an opinion around:

- Those in insurance, securities, real-estate, and business services make on average $75,419 (nat'l avg $68,273—an increase of $7,146, or 11%)
- Those English degree holders working as top- and mid-level managers, executives, and administrators have an annual salary of $70,706 (nat'l avg $74,051—a shortfall of $3,345 per year, or 4.5%)

- Those in sales make $41,134 (nat'l avg $52,378—a whopping shortfall of $11,244 per year, 22% of the overall average of sales wages)
- Other management-related jobs, $48,508 (nat'l avg $51,921)
- Other administrative jobs, $33,777 (vs. $34,547)

A number of obvious considerations come to bear here. First of all, we see that English majors work in all these industries, in significant numbers. Second, they do better in some areas—strictly in terms of salary—and worse in others (much worse, for whatever reason, in sales). Less obviously, the wage gap between women and men also needs to be considered here (by most estimates 77 cents on the dollar) in that the majority of English majors are women.

Looking at career areas in which English majors have higher salaries than the norm, we find insurance, securities, real-estate, and business services. I begin with insurance because of its pervasive place in all our lives. English majors have long staffed the ranks of the insurance industry from top to bottom, and yet very few, even in the industry, are aware of just why that is so. In 2006, Professor Michael Theil, a professor of Risk Management and Insurance Studies at the Vienna University of Economics asked me very directly why I believed that students of English literature succeed in America in the insurance industry. I told him that because insurance is an invisible product, a state of protection against loss, it is especially difficult to explain to its customer base. An insurance *agent*, the front line of the industry, needs to be able to communicate with all sorts of people—educated and uneducated, old and young, kind and unkind—and an agent needs to be able to maintain an account when the product does not perform the way the customer expected it would. The world of insurance is an especially emotional one, coming to people's aid when their loved ones die, when their homes burn down, when their children suffer bodily injury from auto accidents. A gifted insurance agent does not explain the product and walk away; insurance is managed by people in trusted relationship with their clients, and that trust requires all the skills of the English major. Professor Theil commented that my argument made great sense, but he remarked as well that he had never heard anyone speak that way back in Austria about the skills and preparedness of literature majors.

Likewise, securities—stocks and bonds—is an industry that employs scores of English majors every year, and again, here is an industry where the client base needs to trust that their financial advisers can explain why their earnings are wisely invested. It is not enough to make the investment and to monitor its up-and-down ride though the market; the financial manager needs to report persuasively as to *why* those investments work as they do.

Real-estate, too, requires a tremendous amount of interpersonal skill and communication savvy. Real-estate, in its very nature, is always uncertain. Everywhere, at all times, a property is only worth what a qualified buyer is willing to pay. If the sale of homes were easy, we would all sell our own properties, but it is a difficult and thorny process, often fraught with disappointment and anger, and again it requires the ability to listen well to buyers and to their brokers, to negotiate alternative points of view about the value of properties, and to communicate with every type of person.

English majors also thrive in the world of business services, an especially amorphous part of our economy. These are the businesses that serve business—equipment support, consultancy, head-hunters, benefits companies. In all these career areas, business-service companies build strong relationships with their clients, and they have to express in person and in writing exactly why their services are better for their clients than those of their competitors.

In all the other job categories listed in the survey data above, English majors' salaries are within a normal range; some are on average a bit lower, but not dramatically so, especially taking into account the wage-gap between men and women. The one area where we see English majors with significantly suppressed salaries is in jobs defined primarily as "sales." Why English majors should show a drop of 22% over the national average is anyone's guess. Sales salaries typically reflect commission, and it may be that English majors steer away from industries with the insecurity of a commission structure. It may also be that English majors in sales are too "bookish" and introverted or that they do not cope with rejection as well as their peers in the industry. Perhaps they are negatively affected by Arthur Miller's dispirited play *Death of a Salesman* or e.e. Cummings's petulant poem "A salesman is an it that stinks." All we can say with any certainty is that English majors make much less money than the national average in the area of sales.

The Februrary 8, 2006 issue of CNN/Money.com ran an article titled, "Most Lucrative College Degrees: the class of 2004 is faring well, with a special nod to English majors." The journalist was apparently pleased to find that the average starting pay of English majors had risen a full 8.1 percent to $31,113—$2,883 more than the starting pay for Psychology majors and $769 more than that of History majors. English majors, though, do choose to earn less money, at first, than their business-major friends. In 2005, they made $3,599 less than the starting salaries of Marketing majors and much less than the $41,058 average starting salary of an Accounting major.

In the years since 2004, the NACE Salary Survey has shown that entry-level salaries across the disciplines in the liberal arts and sciences have shown a small, steady gain:

Major	2004	2005	2006	2007	2008	2009
English	$31,113	$31,451	$31,385	$31,924	$35,453	$36,604
History	$30,344	$31,739	$33,071	$35,092	$38,056	$38,445
Psychology	$28,230	$30,073	$30,369	$31,857	$34,095	$34,573
Sociology	$29,168	$31,368	$31,096	$32,161	$35,434	$34,290
Biology	$29,629	$31,713	$32,880	$33,944	$35,522	$33,706

The data above indicate that English majors can expect to begin their careers with an average starting salary in the mid 30s, like many of their peers in other LAS disciplines. English majors choose to make a little less when they start out than they would have had they chosen to major in business administration, finance, or economics. They do not, by any means, make a choice to be unemployable or otherwise to live below the poverty line. More important, they make that choice for many good reasons, chief among them being their giftedness at commnication and analysis, their creativity, and their love of reading—all qualities that over time will help them to close the salary gap with which they begin their careers.

Looking to the Future as a Senior

I chose to begin my examination of working English majors with CEOs simply to address those traditional skeptics who might doubt the ability of an English major to succeed in business at all. One does not need to be a "top earner" or a Chief Executive Officer, of course, to be a success in business. Nonetheless, in order to reach any level of success, in order to make any substantial contribution to the general good, an English graduate needs to get that first entry-level job. That frightening first step is the great mystery, the bridge from college English into an actual career path.

At my university, some of my colleagues and I have addressed this issue of uncertainty by transforming our "Senior Project" course in English from one more research project in literary study into something one might aptly sub-title "Get a job!" Students are asked to use all their skills in research, writing, and analysis to investigate what it is they want to do after graduation. We ask that our graduating students assess their own gifts and ambitions and that they think long and hard about what they will do next and why. Our students' career interests in the last ten years reflect the national norms: most students plan to pursue a wide variety of careers in business (retail, public relations, marketing, publishing, etc.); roughly a third of them plan to teach high-school English; and a significant number plan to go on to graduate or professional school, with less than 1% of students pursuing a Ph.D. in English over the last forty years.

Over the semester, the students compile and analyze as much information as they can on their targeted career field (or fields), they network as best they can with people working in that area, they research and actually apply for jobs, and they then write up their work in a binder for the use of future English majors with similar career plans. In the last five years, students have gone on to graduate programs in counseling, public administration, English, acting, stage management, library science, technical writing, and psychology. Many have gone on to law school. Some have taken work in international business; some have stayed local. Some students have had options from multiple companies, including lucrative signing bonuses, while they were still enrolled in courses at Bradley.

By the time they reach their senior year, many of our students have worked in the summer, not to gain experience relevant to a career move but simply to help pay for the expense of a private education. Thus, in the fall and spring, our seniors often do look for paid and unpaid internships somehow related to the career goals they identify in their Senior Project course. They volunteer as grant-writers or researchers for local non-profits; they intern in advertising, marketing, and public relations; some have worked in such narrowly defined disciplines as human resources and global purchasing. Others have sought experience in copy-editing or in web-publishing. Having discovered long ago how important it is for our majors to demonstrate their skills in a workplace of some kind, my department created a course in the major specifically designed to give students *English* credit for their efforts to apply their skills in a constructive way. We call the course "Practicum in English," and it often turns out to be a critically important part of a student's overall college degree, the one place where their English curriculum ties directly in to a specific career opportunity.

A Case Study in How to Get Started

The first key to such success in moving on to one's "apprenticeship" as an English major is for the student to know what his or her special gifts and interests are and how those gifts can be put to productive use. My former student Nicki May is a typical example. She came to Bradley as a Business major, but she felt stifled by the rote memorization of concepts and information she encountered at first, and so she looked for a major that encouraged more creative thinking and independent problem solving, and she found those things in English. Having discovered a love of Economics, however, even at the freshman level, she kept a Business Studies minor and tailored that curriculum to include as much Economics as possible. By the time she was a senior, she knew that she wanted to work in the non-profit sector, so in her research for her Senior Project course, she began to explore the websites of hundreds of non-profit organizations, at which point she noticed that every website she came across listed its corporate and foundation sponsors.

Having identified a list of corporations that sponsored those non-profit companies, Nicki then researched each of those sponsoring businesses and discovered a type of career she had never heard of before: something known on the non-profit side as "corporate giving" and on the corporate side as "cause marketing" or "community relations." These are the divisions of major corporations that make large donations to build up communities in meaningful ways, thus putting forward a positive public face by genuinely doing tremendous good in such areas as literacy, healthcare for the needy, and arts programming. Working in this area seemed to Nicki an excellent way to synthesize her dual interests in creative business and in non-profit service to the community.

Having discovered a suitable career goal, Nicki then began reading in the trade journals in Community Relations and Corporate Giving—reading which in turn made it more clear that such work was perfect for an English major—and she went on to and identified all the available jobs in Corporate Community Relations. That nation-wide research turned up a good number of entry-level jobs, but she discovered a paid internship program at the Target Corporation that appealed to her for a number of important reasons more than any other opportunity. For one thing, she had no corporate experience as a senior in college, and this internship program offered a diverse array of training and tasks. Nicki interviewed with Target in early March and was offered the position by mid-month, long before many of the application deadlines for the other jobs she was considering, and she was very happy to accept the job with two months yet to go before graduation.

That summer, Nicki worked in the Target corporate headquarters in Minneapolis, and in that 12-week internship, she used every skill an English major brings to the table, including her skills in internet and library research. She was tasked, for instance, to determine what corporate giving other companies were currently contributing to the Twin Cities areas--not to see how Target might compete in any way, but to see what social needs might still be left unmet.

Nicki's research that first summer out of college was primarily in the area of educational giving. One of her major projects was to present a report to the entire Community Relations team on the current state of education throughout Minnesota, with a special emphasis on the role of corporations in supporting educational goals. In the process, she used a number of database research tools, including *Foundation Search*, to collect accurate and up-to-date information on educational giving. She also spoke in person and on the phone with educators and educational administrators at many levels. She then synthesized the key points into a PowerPoint presentation for Target's key decision makers. Her job was not to make recommendations, but to give the executive decision makers all the information they needed in order to make an informed decision on how best to endow the community.

That kind of experience—that blend of research, critical thinking, writing, oral reporting, and interpersonal listening—is just the kind of opportunity English majors need to seek out in order to prove that their skills are viable in any given world of work. Whether a student works in such familiar fields as marketing, public relations, human resources, customer service, and sales, or whether one starts out in such unfamiliar territory as "legislative monitoring" or "cause marketing," an English major needs a set of tasks with which to demonstrate his or her ability to gather information, analyze it, and present it in useful ways. In the classroom, English students read things, they think deeply about what they read, and then they present their original ideas in oral and written form. In their actual careers, they do much the same thing; the only thing that changes is the nature of the texts.

Nicki May's decision to try an internship is not unusual, by any means. More and more corporations are now hiring primarily, if not exclusively, from such internal internship programs, and progressive colleges are steering their humanities majors toward those programs. Her internship experience with Target was, however, especially positive and enriching. Through her internship, Nicki met a number of inspiring people who gave her valuable feedback and many, many opportunities to use her skills and to experiment with new ways of thinking. Her supervisors listened to her and encouraged her to be a better listener herself. And at the end of her internship, she was offered an excellent job with the company as an entry-level business analyst in the for-profit side of Target's operations, and though she greatly enjoyed her work at Target, her desire to stay in non-profit work led her to move in another direction.

Knowing that Target had no job openings in Community Relations as her internship came to an end, Nicki applied for a large number of jobs through the Minnesota Council of Non-Profits, a very well-run website that daily posts over a dozen jobs in all areas of non-profit work. Out of those jobs—from public relations positions to direct-service positions with youth organizations—Nicki accepted an offer from AmeriCorps, with a salary cut of 75% compared to the offer she received from Target.

Nicki's new position was to work as a "Promise Fellow" for one year. She chose this position in order to broaden her experience by working directly with the clients of a non-profit and by being directly involved in the management of a program. Her charge as a Promise Fellow was to serve as the resource and support person for students from targeted locations in inner-city Minneapolis, students who were bussed out to the most high-performing middle school in the state. Many of these students were refugees from Kenya, Somalia, Ethiopia, and Togo, and Nicki's job was to help them make the adjustment to all aspects of suburban middle-school life.

When she first started, very little of Nicki's position was pre-determined. In fact, 90% of what she did was of her own initiative, allowing her the freedom to be creative and to use all her English-major skills. She coordinated transportation, especially for those activities outside the regular school day, and she developed after-school programs, mostly for academic support. She also started a breakfast program that had not existed before because the school had never before had enough students who qualified for mandatory free or reduced-price lunch.

Once the year was up, and the grant dollars were no longer available, an administrator at the district office valued Nicki's work enough to find funds to continue her position and to increase her level of responsibility. In the new position, she was asked to build on what she had been doing, and to take on new responsibilities as an advocate. In her new duties, she became involved in district-wide strategic planning; she served on the district's diversity council; and she advocated not only for families from inner-city Minneapolis but also for all open-enrolled students, those students who come to her school from other districts.

In the particular situation of Nicki May's successful transition from English major to gainfully employed educational advocate, we see a few very important key elements:

1. Her initial job search was very broad.
2. She chose jobs that would allow her to demonstrate her skills.
3. She chose jobs that she knew would bring her personal satisfaction.
4. She showed creativity and personal initiative.
5. She showed the ability to communicate with a diverse array of people.
6. She demonstrated the ability to take on increasing levels of responsibility.

That last point—demonstrable growth in responsibility—may be the most important aspect of any English major's unique apprenticeship period. When an English graduate is ready to move on to jobs that require previous work experience, employers will ask them to show how their earlier work demonstrates that they are the kind of employees who will grow into a position. They want to see that their job applicants have proven that they can be trained and re-trained as the nature of the industry changes and develops. Often, what a job applicant has done, exactly, is not nearly as important as what kind of character that person has shown. Is that person a life-long learner, for instance, and can that person bring fresh ideas to the team and grow as an employee? The answer to these questions is often much more important than what tasks that person completed or what equipment that person has operated.

The Importance of Accepting Uncertainty

English majors and their families can do themselves a great favor by coming to terms with the fact that the years *after* graduation, and not those before, determine the nature of a person's career path. For the vast majority of majors, it is impossible to know until senior year what direction they will take after graduation, when the available jobs actually begin to come into view. English majors and their families need to embrace that uncertainty with the confidence that comes from knowing that creative, analytical people with excellent interpersonal and communication skills are always welcome in the work-force.

Dick Moy, the founding Dean of Southern Illinois University Medical School, once spoke to a group of English majors at Bradley about career possibilities in healthcare. He told them that opportunities will come their way much like the old carnival game in which rubber ducks float past children who reach in with a net to discover what prize number is penned underneath their duck. Dr. Moy had come to Bradley at my student's invitation, in part, because he hoped to inspire some young people in the humanities to get involved in the great ethical questions facing the American people today in terms of healthcare—including healthcare rationing and the swelling ranks of the uninsured. He wanted to assure our majors that the opportunities are there, that the need is clearly there for skilled humanists not just in the healthcare industry, but in any industry. "The ducks are in a row," he said, "but you need to know that they are there for you, and you need to be prepared to grab one when the time comes."

CHAPTER 2:

Understanding the English Major's Skill Set

Any career advisor will confirm that companies do not come to college campuses and recruit English majors by virtue of the term papers they wrote in their literature classes. They do not ask students for portfolios of their analyses of Renaissance drama or Victorian fiction. Instead, they come looking for English majors because they have faith that these students will bring a specific set of skills to their workplace, skills that their employees cannot be expected to pick up on the job. For our purposes, I will continue to use the rather stuffy expression "the English skill set" to describe these qualities that make English majors hirable. For companies that do *not* yet openly recruit English majors, it is all the more incumbent upon the English graduates to be able to speak to employers about these very skills that make them employable in the first place and thus to sell themselves to a prospective employer.

Stated simply, English majors read things, they think deeply about what they read, and then they share their thoughts with others in writing and in the spoken word. With that basic process in mind, I break out the English skill set into the following five-part pattern:

- *Analytical Skills*: The ability to think through what we learn from listening, from reading, and from observation.
- *Oral Communication Skills*: The ability to speak comfortably, clearly, concisely, and appropriately to any kind of individual or group.
- *Interpersonal Skills*: The ability to get along with all kinds of people—individually and as part of a team—regardless of differences in cultural values or in personality.
- *Writing Skills*: The ability to commit information and ideas to writing in ways that meet the particular needs of diverse audiences in any kind of situation.
- *Research Skills*: The ability to seek out answers to questions with a critical eye to the credibility of the sources of the information discovered.
- *Computer Skills*: The ability to express ideas and information via computer, with special emphasis on the use of images and graphics in support of text.

There is no way any one person can completely master any one of these sub-skills. Nonetheless, these are the skills that English majors employ in the classroom daily, and taken as a whole, they are the very reason that English majors succeed handily in the world of business in such large numbers. These same skills are, of course, the end-product of any good program in the Liberal Arts (e.g. History, Foreign Language, Religious Studies, Philosophy), but the particular means by which students develop these skills in the classroom is unique to each of the disciplines. This chapter will preliminarily look at the way we work on these skills specifically in the discipline of English, and the next section of this book examines the different aspects of classroom practice that help students develop their skills.

Analysis: Critical Thinking and the Open Mind

The expression "critical thinking" has become such a buzzword over the last twenty years that college freshmen sometimes roll their eyes when asked to define it. Nonetheless, it does identify the lynchpin of the English major's skills. Critical thinking, as I understand it, refers to our ability to look at a text or a situation from multiple points of view; it requires a person to be able to step outside his or her own interpretive lenses and to see an issue as others see it. Anyone can look at a text from one logical or cultural viewpoint, but it takes a critical thinker to see exactly how another group of people could come to see that text differently or how other modes of logic can lead to separate conclusions.

Let's take something as familiar as Elizabeth Barrett Browning's famous sonnet, "How do I love thee? Let me count the ways." In line 8 she writes, "I love thee purely, as men turn from Praise." For decades, I read this line, as most others have, to mean that the speaker's love was "pure," as are the hearts of the humble who "turn away" from praise that others offer them. Without examining my reading critically, I accepted at face value that Barrett Browning was implicitly confirming that the inability to accept praise is somehow an aspect of human "purity." Yet were I to examine that assumption even from my own set of values, I would find it utterly pathological, believing as I do that the inability to accept praise is by definition an expression of human unhappiness, if not a form of low-grade mental illness.

In 1998, one of my students was shocked to see that I and all her classmates had read the line this way at all. She had interpreted it completely differently, and she had no idea that our reading was even possible. What she saw was how the act of praising another purifies and uplifts the one who offers praise. In her specific reading, she envisioned someone turning away from a church service, having just offered praise to God, with a purified heart—not someone with low self-esteem saying, "Aw shucks folks, I'm unworthy." Examining each reading critically, we agreed as a class that the "shucks folks" reading was more in line with what we knew of the author's life, as well as with the other poems in the collection that speak to a low self-image. Nevertheless, we also found the second reading to be both beautiful and illuminative, and no one wanted to deny their classmate the right to her interpretation, nor the author the possibility that she meant it that way all along.

What we see in this simple controversy is that a critical mind is open to alternative interpretation of texts. Critical thinkers remain skeptical that they have the complete picture of anything. True critical thinkers *want* to be told how their views fall short, how alternative views allow for new possibilities. The discipline of college English is not a solitary pursuit. It cannot be pursued in a social void, nor can it be done in a traditional correspondence course. It is not about you and the text; it is about the reading community and the text. Each reader kicks into the kitty his or her own individual insights, but those thoughts are then examined along with those of other classmates, along with the professor's, and often along with the views of scholars of today and of years long past. As Stanley Fish neatly states it, English majors "negotiate truth claims."

Over the course of a four-year degree program, after interpreting complex literature from thousands of alternative points of view—discussion after discussion, article after article, book after book—an English major develops an openness to alternative views as an intellectual habit. That habit is itself a foundation for any creative approach to change or growth, regardless the situation, and it is invaluable in a business leader. When any working unit meets within a company to identify problems and look for solutions, when any manager looks for new ways to increase profits or to improve efficiency, the people involved have to offer and to listen to ideas outside the classic category of "The way we've always done things." Such critical moments of growth and development in business require creativity of thought as well as tolerance of ideas outside the standard comfort zone of thought within the group.

Oral Communication: Speaking Our Minds

Although no major curriculum helps students develop this skill as well as a program in speech communications, few academic programs develop students' public-speaking skills as actively as English. For one thing, English is not typically taught in a lecture format (though in lower-level classes, large state schools sometimes have lecture days followed by T.A. discussion sections). The discipline is simply not about acquiring a body of knowledge by reading books or by watching videos of lectures. Knowledge for us is simply not that static. Given that each student's critical thinking is a central part of the course content, every English major is required to share his or her thinking out loud—both as the person instigating a process of thought and as one of the many classroom "critics" supporting or disagreeing with a stated point of view. English majors routinely speak their minds in front of a group of thinkers, from small seminars (6-12 students) to a typical class size in the mid twenties. In the classroom, every day, it's what they do.

From freshman composition courses, to upper-level courses in Business Communications, to courses in Shakespeare or Sylvia Plath, English majors often have to work in small groups and report their group findings to the class as a whole. Less commonly, students might do a semester-long research project and have to report on the project orally at the end of the semester. More often than not, technically savvy students present their projects with some type of presentation software—usually PowerPoint—but as things stand today, the primary place where English majors develop their presentation and large-group presentation skills will be in the "speech" course or courses required in the general-education curriculum of their college or university.

Of all the skills that comprise the English skills set, public speaking is the one area that students and faculty alike most easily neglect—as other curricula often fail to include the kind of writing assignments that all majors need. Not all English courses require formal in-class presentations, for instance, but oral class-participation is almost always a graded aspect of any English course design. That the oral-language side of English is just one aspect among many works out well, in that many types of people choose to major in English, and many types of jobs are available to them, some that require very little public speaking, some that require a great deal (a data research job, for instance, versus a job in public relations or marketing). English faculty respect the quiet, "bookish" English major, as well as the confident student with a hand up for every question, but almost universally, every English major is regularly challenged to present his or her ideas orally in an open discussion with peers.

Interpersonal Skills: How We Know Who We Know

English majors grow in their interpersonal skill level in two basic ways: 1) they learn how other people think and feel through their interactions in class and 2) they learn how people very different from themselves think and feel by reading literature in which they put themselves in the shoes of fictional characters of different eras, different genders, different cultures, different stages of life, different sexual orientations, different ideologies. Both approaches to seeing the world through the eyes of others are effective, and the desired outcome of such education is a person of greater empathy, a person who wants to know what other people are thinking and feeling—a person less capable of treating others in the workplace or in the broader society as objects.

From the social nature of the guided-discussion approach to the English classroom, students grow in their understanding of others. If an English classroom reflects the diversity of American society—racially, ethnically, religiously, politically—if each student is truly free to share his or her understanding of texts, free from the fear of either political correctness or conservative group-think, those students will grow in their understanding of the way people think who are *different* from them. Ideally, English majors find that in sharing their deep-seated views on issues very important to them (issues of social justice, religious truth, concepts of the beautiful or the tragic) they form friendships with people whom they might otherwise not have ever engaged in such a way. And in such friendship, intellectual friendship that explores issues of cultural depth, they come to see in a very healthy way how others see the world.

I have three examples of such "Odd Couple" friendship that have inspired me in recent years. One is that between the 19th-century scholars Thomas Henry Huxley and Matthew Arnold; another is the collegial friendship between the two powerful federal congressmen Dan Rostenkowski and Bob Michel; and the third is the friendship between two contemporary political writers, Cal Thomas and Bob Beckel. These people's ability to pursue a greater truth by bringing together seemingly exclusive points of view, while yet holding on to a respectful personal friendship, should itself be understood as a discrete skill—one, again, invaluable in the real world of work and critically important in the crafting of the laws that shape American life.

The first of these friendships began toward the end of the 1860s, when the poet and essayist Matthew Arnold began to express his strong views that the study of literature was fundamental to the development of civilized society. Of special interest to him at that time was the importance of literature to the fabric of the new English and American public schools and universities. In the course of that aspect of his career as a writer and public speaker—that of educational policy advocate—he locked horns with his friend, the scientist Thomas Henry Huxley, Aldous Huxley's grandfather. Huxley had been traveling widely, arguing for the importance of a sound scientific education as the necessary bedrock of a college education. He gave the inaugural addresses at both Johns Hopkins University and the Scientific College at Birmingham, for instance, arguing in his essay *Science and Culture* that scientific education had to take on a greater role in education everywhere, openly directing his words in opposition to Arnold's argument that literary education is key to the understanding of culture:

> I find myself wholly unable to admit that either nations or individuals will really advance, if their common outfit draws nothing from the stores of physical science. I should say that an army, without weapons of precision and with no particular base of operations, might more hopefully enter upon a campaign upon the Rhine than a man, devoid of a knowledge of what physical science has done in the last century, upon a criticism of life.

It is important to note that Huxley did not argue against the study of literature *per se*, but only against his perception that Arnold and others considered literary study *sufficient* to a citizen's understanding of the world.

Three years after Huxley's 1880 address, Arnold toured America on a lecture circuit, again openly debating Huxley's public declarations about the role that scientific education should play relative to traditional studies in literature, both classical and modern. One of Arnold's lectures, "Literature and Science," appears in his 1885 collection *Discourses in America*, and in it Arnold continues his back-and-forth with Huxley:

> At present it seems to me, that those who are for giving to natural knowledge, as they call it, the chief place in the education of the majority of mankind, leave one important thing out of their account: the constitution of human nature.

Arnold came to argue not that literature alone was a sufficient education for late 19th century English and American citizens, but that people would need literary study all the more "as they have the more and the greater results of science to relate to the need in man for conduct, and the need in him for beauty." His key point in the essay was that every person has an innate need to relate all the various parts of their knowledge into one coherent ethical and moral whole, and he saw *literature* classes as the means for people to examine the human experience through moral and ethical lenses.

Huxley and Arnold made history in their adversarial, often contentious debate over the proper place of scientific vs. literary education, but their audiences could not know at the time what we now know from their surviving letters: that amid all their intense public argument, they remained intimate friends. For me, the most moving evidence of that friendship is a letter that Huxley wrote to Arnold when his own bad health had taken him to the warmer climate of Egypt. Arnold's 18-year-old son, Trevenen, had died at the end of the winter of 1872 (Arnold's younger son Thomas, then sixteen, had died four years earlier), and Huxley wrote to his friend the following words of consolation in a letter from Thebes dated March 10th, 1872:

> My dear Arnold—I cannot tell you how shocked I was to see in the papers we re-
> ceived yesterday the announcement of the terrible blow which has fallen on Mrs.
> Arnold and yourself.
>
> Your poor boy looked such a fine manly fellow the last time I saw him, when
> we dined at your house, that I had to read the paragraph over and over again before
> I could bring myself to believe what I read. And it is such a grievous opening of
> a wound hardly yet healed that I hardly dare to think of the grief which must have
> bowed down Mrs. Arnold and yourself.
>
> I hardly know whether I do well in writing to you. If such trouble befell me
> there are very few people in the world from whom I could bear even sympathy—but
> you would be one of them, and therefore I hope that you will forgive a condolence
> which will reach you so late as to disturb rather than soothe, for the sake of the hearty
> affection which dictates it.

What we see in this letter is the depth of the human relationship that was always a frame to Arnold and Huxley's public arguments about education policy, at the critical moment in history when education began the process of displacing some of the classical education that had to be removed to make room for courses in theoretical and applied science. I suggest that they were able to enter so deeply into the debate, and so successfully, not in spite of their friendship but because of it.

In a similar vein, the former U.S. Congressman from Illinois, Bob Michel, has spoken publicly with nostalgia for the days when politicians could talk in friendship across the aisle. Dan Rostenkowski, the former Chairman of the House Ways and Means Committee (which holds the purse strings to Congress) recalled in an August 16th, 1998 article in the *Chicago Tribune Magazine* how he, Bob Michel, and Republican Congressman Harold Collier would travel to and from D.C. together in one car:

> When I first went to Congress we'd drive home every weekend, Bob Michel and me,
> and Harold Collier driving. . . . We always had great cooperation between Democrats
> and Republicans in the Illinois delegation. We couldn't have gotten all that we got
> without both sides.

Rostenkowski was one of the most powerful figures in the Democratic party—Michel and Collier in the Republican opposition—but they were friends, and their friendship was indom- itable. They demonstrated that crucial skill of separating the act of critical thinking, especial- ly when their values led them to adversarial conclusions, from their ability to communicate together as friends.

We can see this same thing again in the 2007 book *Common Ground*, jointly authored by the two diametrically opposed political writers, Cal Thomas and Bob Beckel. Their book argues anew for the critical importance of civil, respectful disagreement between the political voices of our time. Thomas and Beckel publicly argue about their personal vision of what is right and wrong, true or false in American politics, but they do so as friends—not because they see their contention as a cynical game, but because they respect one another's right to disagree in good conscience. That respect is absolutely essential to the discipline of English. Class discussion cannot proceed in a productive way if the professor does not respect the alternative views of the students, nor if the students are not seeking out the alternative points of view of their classmates, their professors, and their literary-critical reading. We need to realize that analytical skills are necessarily tied to interpersonal skills. Without the ability to communicate respectfully with people who disagree with our views, intellectual *growth* would be, by definition, impossible. Furthermore, what would remain would merely be a growth in demagoguery.

Writing Skills: Matching the Message to the Audience and Situation

Nearly every entry-level job for which an English major can apply will list "excellent writing skills" as a specific requirement for hiring, but the question still remains of exactly what business and industry mean by the expression "writing skills." We are safe in assuming, however, that they are not asking for the five-paragraph essay so familiar to the Baby Boom generation, nor are they asking for students to be able to write research papers in literature with proper MLA documentation. Again, the expository writing required in English classes is not an end in itself, but only a means to an end. By spending a few thousand hours inside and outside of class formulating original ideas and sharing them in writing, English majors develop levels of writing skill that simply cannot be taught without that heavy investment of time and a great deal of individualized feedback from faculty. The goal is a facility with language that allows an English graduate to write prose that is 1) clear, 2) concise, 3) complete, 4) punctual, and 5) appropriate for the given audience and situation.

When people I meet in the business world find out that I am an English professor, they commonly respond with a remark like "Uh oh," or "I better watch my grammar then." At some level, people carry the idea that grammatical "correctness" is at the heart of the discipline of English and that English teachers are in the habit of correcting others' spoken English. Grammar is typically what people outside the discipline of English assume that writing instruction is ultimately about, in part perhaps because managers see so many letters, memos, and reports with atrocious grammar (comma splices, subject-verb disagreements, sentence fragments, non-parallel series, etc.). For managers, good grammar is a part of the professional public face of a company, and they cannot afford to have public documents circulating that make the company's workforce appear poorly educated. Good grammar is akin to professional dress or to a clean and welcoming lobby.

Given, then, that grammar is very important in the working world, there is a disconnect here with college English. Decades of academic studies have gone to show that grammar can only be taught in an effective way in the context of writing. All that research concurs that grammatical drills in a vacuum, without the application of grammatical principles in writing assignments, provide only short-term knowledge at best and do not in the end lead students to craft their sentences with significant grammatical command. Unfortunately, this can sometimes be reduced to "I don't have to teach grammar because it will come naturally to the students over time as they write." More often, however, professors take the time to mark the grammatical errors on students' papers and communicate in the context of that writing what the student has yet to learn.

Nevertheless, grammar is understood in all English departments as one of the least important, yet necessary, aspects of our teaching. The central goal of writing instruction in almost all English curricula can be summarized as "clarity of communication appropriate to a given audience in a given situation." In addition, writing instruction also focuses on the research and critical thinking that go into having something worth communicating in the first place. Composition classes therefore force writers to discover what they think in a protracted process of pre-writing, drafting, revising, editing, and proofreading—not because all writing situations will allow that kind of time, but because our most important and original thinking requires a process of critical thought. Grammar comes along as a welcome guest in those larger aspects of our teaching.

Fundamentally, a skilled writing major is able to read an audience and shape a message in line with that audience's needs. Without a clear understanding of the audience, writers cannot know if they have given enough examples to support a point; they cannot know if any one example is persuasive in the first place. Without a knowledge of audience, the writer cannot know if the word choice is too learned, too informal, or too ideologically loaded. To illustrate this point, my first year of teaching took place in a small town in the mountains of western Maine, and this town operated its city government in the "Townhall" tradition of New England: once a year, all the concerned townspeople would gather in a large meeting space and take turns talking through issues at one central microphone. At the particular meeting I attended, the issue of insufficient student parking came up, and my university president stood up to address the town. Asked when the university would provide enough campus parking that students would no longer be parking up residential neighborhood streets, my president said something along the lines of, "I have a team of experts studying the situation, and we will keep seeking solutions until the problem has been mitigated."

A haggard gentleman apparently in his early 70s then walked up to the microphone, waving his hands and exclaiming very loudly, "Well excu-u-u-se me mister doctor president if some of us here don't know what the word *mitigated* means!" The president's face then turned visibly red, and the crowd broke out in raucous laughter. The curmudgeon who complained about the president's polysyllabic word turned out to be a Harvard-trained attorney whose apparent purpose in speaking at all had been to embarrass the president for not being ready to match his diction to the audience at hand.

Although the trained writer needs to be sensitive to the nature of audience, there are elements of writing situations that have less to do with audience and more to do with other aspects of the situation. In the world of business, for instance, time is more precious than it is in the life of a college student. While it is true that when people in business discover

I teach English, their initial response is often "Uh oh," one manager had a memorable and instructive response. He said, "Look, could you teach them how to write fast? I get all these college graduates who think I have all day for them to finish a report, when I actually need it in fifteen minutes." On the surface, this "need for speed" in writing seems counter-current to the standard approach in the English classroom, which is a process-oriented series of drafts and revisions, yet in the end, the only way to develop the skills required to write both quickly and well is through years of slow, laborious writing in which every writer's unique problems come to the surface under the watchful eye of someone who can explain the nature of the problem and offer workable alternatives. Musicians learn to play scales quickly through years of slow, laborious practice and dogged instruction; so it is, too, with writers.

Research Skills: Seeking Information in the Computer Age

English majors need to be experienced researchers for a very simple reason: they are not allowed to assert points in their writing without grounding those points in reasoned evidence. If they write about a literary text, they support their points with specifics from the text; if they write about society, they ground their points in sociological study; if they write about religion, they seek out evidence in theology and sacred text. No subject should be off-limits in the composition courses that comprise an enormous part of the college English curriculum. Students write research-based essays on psychology, philosophy, women's issues, sports, popular culture, history; they engage hot-button issues in medical ethics, politics, and social justice. Sometimes students are given pre-determined research topics, but often they are asked to choose a topic that moves them somehow, both intellectually and emotionally, and to come to a deeper understanding of that issue in the process of research and revision.

Thus English majors are directed to a large variety of research tools, and they are expected the learn how to differentiate a legitimate source from an illegitimate one, a biased source from a more objective one, or a persuasive source from a non-persuasive one, regardless their legitimacy. It is not enough to locate information; an English major has to evaluate that information, abstract that which is relevant to an argument, and present that information in a manner appropriate for the given audience and situation. Research skills in the humanities—as in the social sciences—are not merely mechanical, they are in their foundation intellectual.

There is, nonetheless, an important set of skills that an English major needs in order to ferret out information in the many venues in which they write. Luckily for them, an army of trained information scientists is out there to help. In the course of four years, all English majors necessarily have to seek out the help of reference librarians when they cannot find what they were looking for. The college reference librarians on every campus do not simply find things for students, they take every opportunity to train students in the research techniques necessary to provide the given information. In my own undergraduate experience, we were all still working with paper: card catalogues and the Library of Congress Subject Headings Index (two huge hard-bound volumes that listed the key terms under which texts were catalogued). Today the LCHS is still a vital part of the research process, but it is available on-line, along with a myriad of other tools like Webfeat, which allows students to search an enormous volume of indexes simultaneously, and SFX, which makes on-line versions of the text available to any subscriber to the library services, students included.

Every college and university librarian is also a type of teacher (many of them were also undergraduate English majors), but unless students are doing motivated, research-based writing, they will not avail themselves of the skills-based instruction that librarians routinely offer. Some students in other majors will do this only in a freshman English class; others will do research-based writing only within the confines of their narrow discipline, and then very seldom. English majors, on the other hand, have no option but to produce a great deal of source-based writing, and English majors who are aware that they will move toward a career in business should be advised to expand their horizons in the topics they choose to write about and to explore as many different databases as possible.

Computer Skills: The Importance of Visual Rhetoric

In the last twenty years, software programs like Excel, Adobe Photoshop, Dreamweaver, Flash, and Pagemaker revolutionized our ability to enhance our writing with what we in English often refer to as "Visual Rhetoric." Not only can our students now insert captioned photographs in their print documents, they can write cyber-documents that insert streaming video that speaks out loud to the reader. Production lines in factories now have on-line instruction manuals available to workers that not only explain in writing how to perform a function, but also demonstrate the technique visually. Yet there is much more to effective communication in visual rhetoric than simply placing an image or a chart in close proximity to relevant text. In English, we try to train our writers in the ethical use of visual aids, in the clear and coherent integration of text and image, and in the need to give the reader all the data necessary to understand the point at hand.

Our mission in the discipline of English is not to provide the level of expert training that Media Studies majors receive in the mechanics of such program packages as Adobe Creative Suite 4 and the Microsoft Office Suite of products. Nevertheless, we encourage our students to write in electronic media, to turn in assignments as web pages, and to present their research with integrated table, charts, graphs, and images. We help our students design their electronic documents, planning out the way that the language and the visual rhetoric will relate to and support each other.

In recent years, most English majors study visual rhetoric only in upper-level courses in composition, although some colleges offer such instruction at the 100-level. But as professors in the discipline of English continue to develop their own skill levels with multi-media software, students of English can expect to see more overlap and cooperative support between their courses in English and their courses in communications and media studies. Any English major—no matter how skilled he or she is at analysis, oral communication, writing, research, or relating to people—any English major will be made more marketable in the job search if he or she has proven skills with internet software and Microsoft Office.

All six categories of the English skill set come to bear ultimately on a graduate's ability to make good, reasoned decisions in complex areas of thought and to stand by those thoughts when committed to paper, in whatever form of writing might be appropriate. The marketability, the practical *usefulness* then of the English major is always tied to the importance of writing in the workplace, and thus of clear thinking and clear, effective communication.

My Ph.D. advisor, Jack Stillinger, once paraphrased the English positivist philosopher John Stuart Mill as to the three questions, in order, that all good writing answers:

1. Huh? The assertion of an original idea. (Thesis)
2. Oh Yeah? The presentation of evidence that makes the assertion sensible. (Development)
3. So What? The discussion of the relevance of the assertion to the reader. (Conclusion)

The first question demands that the reader have thought deeply about the issue and have developed a relationship with a reader that warrants sharing the idea. It requires both critical thinking skills and interpersonal skills. The second question requires the reader to do the research that provides the evidence and rationale that the reader had not yet engaged. And the third question requires the writer to know and to care about the audience. English, as a discipline, teaches writing in an interpersonal, communal context. When an English major sits down to write, it is to offer the reader something of value — a clearer understanding of an intellectual issue, a new perspective on a moral or ethical issue, a new sensitivity to the social circumstance of a person or a group, a new insight into politics, art, or human relationship. When English professors say that we teach our students to write with a purpose, that purpose is invariably to *help* the reader in some constructive way.

Business communications are little different. In then end, consumers are drawn to a business, relate to that business, and stay with that business because of that company's ability to communicate with them, in good circumstances and bad. Likewise, customers walk away from companies every day because of bad communications, often grounded in a company's inability to relate to that customer's sensibility, whether through ineffective advertising or through poor customer relations. In addition, companies lose customers daily because in the competitive marketplace, some other company came up with a new, creative approach to a product or service and stole their customers away. Creativity, interpersonal understanding, and good writing skills are always welcome in the real world of business. English majors, once they have demonstrated that they can actually use the skills of their discipline, are highly employable.

SECTION II
HOW THE ENGLISH CLASSROOM BUILDS MARKETABLE SKILLS

C H A P T E R 3 :
Literary Study—Negotiating Multiple Points of View

When the great seal of my university was first developed in 1897, the crafters placed "Literature" at the bottom, at the fundament of the structure, flanked above on the left by "Science" and on the right by "Industry." From the very beginning, Lydia Moss Bradley considered literature an essential part of any "practical" education, and yet of all the areas of study we engage in college English, literature is the one that most people perceive as the most useless. What the designers of the Bradley seal considered self-evident truth—the important relationship of literature to science and industry—has often been lost in our generation. In Lydia Moss Bradley's era, literature was considered by many a necessary part of a citizen's growth in virtue. One studied literature to learn essential truths from a fairly short list of the great works by the great writers of the ages. While I would not dismiss the role that reading plays in anyone's moral development, I would limit the scope of discussion to a few key social aspects of literary study one can safely interpret as moral: empathy, collegiality, and a receptive open-mindedness. Any course in literature—whether it was taught in 1922, 1946, or 2010— will help students develop these three key areas of skill, as well as a few others, but in order to understand how, we need to look at what actually happens in the literature classroom that leads students to develop these marketable skills.

Developing Empathy

I begin with empathy because it is the critical component that allows for the other two literary skills (collegiality and open-mindedness). Empathy is not an old word. It was first introduced into English in 1903 as a translation of the German word "Einfühlung," which literally means "projection into something." From its first use in English, it was a term specific to human psychology that expressed a person's ability to "project" him or herself into an object of contemplation. It is that quality of the human imagination that allows us to see what others see and to feel what others feel, regardless how different those people are from us. Without empathy, a writer cannot match a message to an audience, nor can businesses successfully market their goods and services.

In a letter to his close friend Benjamin Bailey (Nov. 22, 1817), the poet John Keats wrote the following detail: "if a sparrow come before my window, I take part in its existence and pick about the gravel." This passage is often referenced as an expression of literary artists' ability to project themselves into others, to live imaginatively in the person of another, and thus to be able to create a convincing world of character and setting.

That same quality of empathy that is so essential in creating literature is also demanded in the act of reading. The influential American philosopher Richard Rorty (1931-2007) wrote about this subject at length in his controversial 1989 book *Contingency, Irony, and Solidarity*. Rorty argues that literature plays an important role in a moral progress toward a greater unity, a great human solidarity, by opening people's eyes to the suffering of others. To clarify what he means by "solidarity," Rorty draws his reader's attention to a little-known fact of Holocaust history:

> If you were a Jew in the period when the trains were running to Auschwitz, your chances of being hidden by your gentile neighbors were greater if you lived in Denmark or Italy than if you lived in Belgium. A common way of describing this difference is by saying that many Danes and Italians showed a sense of human solidarity which many Belgians lacked.

Rorty argues that specific writers and specific texts can help readers overcome cruelties and injustices that they consciously or unconsciously embrace as members of a culture in a given place and time. In chapter seven, he groups these books into two categories: "(1) books which help us see the effects of social practices and institutions on others and (2) those which help us see the effects of our private idiosyncrasies on others." Among the novels he identifies in the first group are Harriet Beecher Stowe's *Uncle Tom's Cabin*, Victor Hugo's *Les Misérables*, Theodore Dreiser's *Sister Carrie*, Radclyffe Hall's *The Well of Loneliness*, and Richard Wright's autobiographical *Black Boy*. All of these books illuminate social injustices in ways that have led readers to distance themselves from cruelties in society that they might have earlier ignored or thoughtlessly embraced. They are all indeed novels that when taught in an English classroom lead to the examination of social justice issues both past and present.

The second group of books Rorty discusses deal more with individual human psychology, rather than with broad social realities, and he shows how a particular character—e.g. Mr. Causaubon in George Eliot's *Middlemarch* or Mrs. Jellyby in Dickens's *Bleak House*—can hold a mirror up to readers and reveal ways in which we are unaware of how our own behavior causes pain or humiliation to other people. Rorty argues that moral progress occurs when we grow in "the ability to think of people wildly different from ourselves as included in the range of 'us.'" In other words, our skill of empathy—our ability to "project in" to the experience of people different from us—prohibits us from acts of cruelty that we might otherwise commit or ignore if we were not schooled by our reading in the human experience of others.

Developing Collegiality

The study of literature is not a quantitative thing. Students are not asked to take in a body of knowledge and report back on multiple-choice tests the factual information they absorbed in their reading. Far from it, they are asked to formulate original insights and to articulate their reaction to the social world they encountered in their reading. They are asked to determine cogent readings of complex works of poetry, fiction, drama, and non-fiction prose, and then they are required to engage in back-and-forth discussion about those ideas in a classroom full of diverse opinion. Any such classroom should be understood as a team, a team of interpreters trying to maximize the power of the text to convey significant meaning. That interpersonal give-and-take of the classroom is at least as important, educationally, as is the reading itself—something anyone can do on his or her own without going to college.

Many interpersonal skills come to bear in this process of negotiating the meaning of literature among a group of readers. One is the ability to restrain your own ego when something someone says offends you. In the classroom, this happens routinely. One student may have ardent views about religion, for instance, that come to bear on a reading, and that view may be completely incompatible with the views of others in the class. The task of the professor, and of the class as a whole, is then to negotiate those differences into a more comprehensive awareness.

The way such discussion actually happens in the classroom is that English professors do not simply lecture. Instead, we direct discussion and contextualize that discussion in light of the long conversation about the literature available in the scholarship we have read or written. Thus, a literature classroom is often conducted in a circle, and students either volunteer a point of view or they are called on to assert their opinion on an issue in the text. Other students then agree or disagree by offering alternative readings of passages in the text at hand, and the professor does the same—not as the high arbiter of truth, but as a senior member of the team looking for new ways of thinking about familiar readings. In the course of such intimate discussion, emotions can often get inflamed.

For example, in Dostoevsky's masterpiece *The Brothers Karamazov*, one of the brothers relates a poem he is writing in which Jesus comes again during the heyday of the Spanish Inquisition. In this chapter of Dostoevsky's novel, the Grand Inquisitor has Christ arrested and then interrogates him in his jail cell the night before he is to be burned in an *auto-da-fé*. He rails against Christ about his irresponsibility in empowering the people to take responsibility for their own spiritual lives, insisting that the Roman Catholic priesthood is necessary to free the people from the unreasonable burden of their own free will. He grows so angry with Jesus that the Roman cleric tells Christ with impassioned intensity that "if anyone deserves our pyre more than all others, it is You."

The "Grand Inquisitor" chapter is so compelling that it is published separately, with diverse commentary; it is written about at great length in the scholarship of many nations; and it is has been taught in philosophy courses as a text in pre-modern existentialism. Wherever it is taught, however, it leads to heated and sometimes angry class discussion. Some see it as unfairly characterizing the Catholic Church; others see it as a perfectly legitimate indictment, even in our time. Others don't see it as critical of any Christian denomination at all, but as a sad assessment of a non-believer's approach to organized religion (this is the younger brother Alyosha's stated view in the chapter, for instance) or as a portrayal of heroic individualism. Regardless, students often weigh in to discussion by drawing upon their own religious background, sometimes with resentment, sometimes with gratitude and praise for the role of religion in their lives. And typically, those alternative views lead to highly sensitive disagreement.

The same kind of heat can be generated when the literature runs to moral issues in sexuality (the comic lewdness of Marvell's "To His Coy Mistress"; the sensitive examination of lesbian life in Hall's *The Well of Loneliness*), or to the deep feelings tied up in the death of those we love (the tragic despair expressed in the poet John Keats's last letters; the grief expressed in the many child-death scenes in Victorian fiction), or to the pain of examining the historical experience of black America from the inside (the sacrifice and horror of slave narratives; the dignity and the injustice found in the literature of the Harlem Renaissance).

It takes students years of practice, years of experience negotiating uncomfortable difference in opinion and sensibility before English majors develop the skill involved in tucking away their egos when classmates criticize or even condemn their own most treasured values. When they do, however, they are much better prepared to do the same thing in the workplace. In virtually any line of work, that skill is invaluable. The expression "The customer is always right," for instance, comes with this skill built in.

When an emotionally distraught patient or family member unloads on a nurse or physician, when an angry customer writes an unreasonable or abusive letter to an insurance agent, when a long-term client of a Fortune-50 company is offended by the inappropriate wording of a letter—the person being addressed has to be able to swallow his or her own pride or self-righteous offense and address the unhappy client with calming respect, defusing the heated emotion of the communication and tactfully bringing the conversation down to the disputed facts of the case. Sometimes it is even necessary to allow the customer to be completely unjust and unreasonable, rather than to damage or destroy the human relationship between that person and the company—whether the dispute come in the context of a hospital, a yarn shop, or an airline company.

Where better to learn such a skill, a skill that has no clear name to identify it, than in a classroom where students argue about those things they care about the most: politics, religion, social justice, art, beauty, and truth? Outside of the parliament building in Vienna, Austria, two statues stand that speak to this very ability. On each side of the front entrance are statues of nude men trying to reign in wild horses. This is to symbolize the importance of both sides of political debate to set aside their resentment and anger and to talk civilly about their differences in hope that political solutions—often matters of imperfect compromise—can be struck for the good of the nation. Perhaps this particular subset of interpersonal skills is best identified as "collegiality," the ability to maintain friendship in the midst of adversarial communications. This is clearly the quality that led President Obama to appoint former Republican Congressman Ray LaHood for his current post as the U.S. Secretary of Transportation.

No matter what word we choose to identify it, the ability to tame our egos and allow other people to disagree with us in good conscience is a vital part of teamwork in any environment. English majors work on that skill every time they venture into the sometimes very messy process of in-class discussion of literature.

Developing an Openness to Alternative Interpretation

As any literature class should teach us to distrust the definitiveness of our own readings, it should also teach us very firmly that the words we use, though we believe we know what we mean when we use them, do not necessarily communicate to others what we think they do. The importance of this simple point to the world of business can easily be underestimated. The very reason why the interpretations of text are always so diverse is that the words themselves, often so seemingly simple on the surface, are much more complex than we are willing to acknowledge.

Let's look, for instance at the Bill of Rights. The words themselves are very simple. The first clause of the First Amendment reads quite simply, "Congress shall make no law respecting an establishment of religion, or prohibiting the free exercise thereof." The entire Second Amendment reads, "A well regulated militia, being necessary to the security of a free state, the right of the people to keep and bear arms, shall not be infringed." The terms themselves are not difficult; the sentence structure is unusual in our time but not inscrutable. Nonetheless, our society continues to struggle in lawsuit after lawsuit to come to terms with the actual application in law of these simple independent clauses.

The interpretation of such simple language has always required, and will always require, supreme court justices to rule in cases in which diverse factions of interpreters struggle for their unique understanding to be enacted as law, rather than their opposition's reading. The long history of judges' decisions then takes on a force through precedents that affect every aspect of the shared rights of American citizens. In recent years alone, five supreme court justices have been undergraduate English majors: William O. Douglas (1939-75); Abe Fortas (1965-69); Potter Stewart (1958-81); Thurgood Marshall (1967-91); and Clarence Thomas (1991-present). As people whose job it is on a daily basis to negotiate between multiple interpretations of texts, all these judges were effectively practicing English majors throughout their professional careers.

The job of a supreme court justice sheds a fascinating light on the multiple-interpretation nature of the English classroom. In literary criticism and theory, some interpretation focuses on what we believe an author *intended* when writing a text; other schools of criticism focus more strictly on the specific language of the text, with all its potential meanings; and other approaches focus on the power of various audiences to *receive* the text in different ways. Simplistically stated, literary criticism tends to focus interpretation on the author, the text, or the reader.

The implications here for the law are enormous. Interpretation of the constitution proceeds in the same way as any textual interpretation. We refer, for instance, to one group of interpretive approaches as "originalism." What we in English refer to as "authorial intention," constitutional theorists refer to as "original understanding": the idea that a constitutional statement should be understood in terms of what the people meant who drafted and ratified the language. In English classes, student and faculty both build arguments routinely as to what we think an author *intended*, often by situating the text in reference to the biographical data available at the time. Often writers will actually indicate what they were trying to say in a letter to a close friend or family member, for instance, or the author might have taken a position in an essay or in a dinner conversation recorded in the diary of a person sitting across the table.

Related to constitutional "originalism," we also have the more common interpretive approach of "original meaning" theory. This approach to interpreting constitutional language tries to determine what educated people at the time of the ratification of the text would have understood the constitution to mean. This, too, is common practice in the English classroom. It is a part of what we refer to as "historical criticism." Without any knowledge of the conditions of the English working class in Victorian England, for instance, one would be hard put to engage the fiction of Charles Dickens. So, too, the novels of Jane Austen take on much deeper meaning the more one understands about the conditions of women in late 18th- and early 19th-century England. Taken together, both interpretive approaches are commonly referred to in English as "historical-biographical" criticism, and though many other approaches to interpretation exist, the historical-biographical approach is almost always in play at some level in an open discussion of literature.

But in the years since W. K. Wimsatt and Monroe Beardsley published their 1946 article "The Intentional Fallacy," those engaged in the discipline of English have been keenly aware of how difficult it is to establish any definitive argument as to authorial intention. Some schools of thought, in fact, have argued that notions of authorial intention are fundamentally irrelevant, in that texts will mean what they mean to readers, regardless of intention. The same is true in constitutional thought. Against the author-based approaches of "originalism," we have what is loosely referred to as "The Living Constitution." These interpretive approaches are more "audience" based—the audience being in this case American society—in that they look at the constitution as evolving over time as our society evolves. The original framers, for instance, intended that slavery be permitted and that women not have the right to vote. Clearly, "authorial intention" has to be placed in a reasoned balance with "audience reception." Our judges look at the same words, come to separate interpretations, and negotiate—amid multiple possibilities—what the words will actually mean in real terms. In constitutional theory, we see with immense clarity how our interpretation of words has monumentally important consequences. Appropriately then, English courses train future judges to see that all interpretive approaches need to be tested and weighed, whether the emphasis be on author, text, or reader. And, not surprisingly, many experts in Constitutional Law— like the former Dean of Stanford's law school, Kathleen Sullivan—have undergraduate degrees in literary study.

In the English classroom, students and faculty struggle together every day to see exactly how it is that the words on the page lead in so many various directions. The poet William Wordsworth's "A Slumber Did My Spirit Seal" is an excellent text with which to see just how complex the simplest words can be:

A Slumber did my spirit seal
I had no human fears.
She seemed a thing that did not feel
The touch of earthly years.
She has no motion now, no force,
She neither sees nor hears,
Rolled round in earth's diurnal course
With rocks, and stones, and trees.

This seemingly simple poem—just eight lines, alternating between eight and six syllables—turns out to be so complex that it is a central focal point of a book-length analysis. Mark Jones's *The 'Lucy Poems': A Case Study in Literary Knowledge* (1994) offers a rich array of interpretive approaches to this poem, as well as to Wordsworth's other short poems about the mysterious "Lucy."

Once a reader negotiates the lines for the first time, a few fundamental questions in reading are inevitable:

1. Who is speaking, and to whom?
2. What is the situation?

In this particular text, neither of these large-scale questions is clearly determined by the words themselves, and in order to answer them, the reader is forced to fill in a great number of blanks. In the process of filling in the gaps in the poem, each reader brings a different set of experiences and values, and the outcomes are therefore incredibly diverse.

The first line alone is profoundly indeterminate. We do not know what the word "slumber" means, for starters; we do not know what "Spirit" means; and we do not know how the verb "to seal" is operating at the end of the line. How we choose to interpret the word "spirit" is immensely important to the overall situation of the poem. One set of readings presumes that the "spirit" is the speaker's soul, or more loosely the speaker's inner self: "My spirit [my soul] is sealed in slumber [shut away in sleep]." Once the reader interprets "My spirit" as the speaker's soul, the nature of the slumber then opens up to a diverse set of basic interpretations:

1. The sleep can be the sleep of death, in which case the speaker is looking at the self from some state of afterlife, much like the speaker of Emily Dickinson's famous poem, "I heard a fly buzz when I died."
2. The sleep can also be more literally "sleep," and the rest of the poem shows the sleeping spirit being examined by the wakeful self.
3. The sleep can be some other kind of "slumbering"—a state of deep meditation, of depression, of grief, even of a state of spiritual death—in which case the poem examines a detached mind examining itself in an altered state.

All these readings require the reader to interpret the word "spirit" as a feminine noun, and thus the reader must be comfortable seeing the "soul," the "mind," the "inner self," as meta-phorically female. Some readers will do this naturally; others will resist such readings.

While one portion of a typical classroom of English majors pursues such readings, an-other will begin their interpretations with the assumption that "my spirit" refers to a beloved woman or to a female child. This assumption, too, leads to another spectrum of readings of its own:

1. Death sealed my beloved in an eternal slumber.
2. Mortality sealed my child in the slumber of death.

And a third group of students will proceed in a hybrid set of readings in which "My spirit" refers to the speaker's inner self, but the "she" in line three does not refer back to that spirit but to the unnamed beloved female.

All of these options go to illustrate that no matter what a writer's intentions might be, the words themselves will be received on the *reader's* terms, not the writer's. To a well-trained English major, this fact is as clear as any in life, and yet in the everyday world of communications, whether in the workplace or in the home, people often assume that the words they speak and the words they write can only be received as they were intended. In seeing over and over that the words they thought at first were both clear and simple are open to radically different interpretation, English majors learn *not* to assume that their own words are clear on the surface. They learn, from their first course in freshman composition, that their audience—not their inner voice—determines whether their writing conveys what they want it to convey.

This aspect of the English skills set, the openness to alternative interpretation, under-pins a more broad open-mindedness, something absolutely essential in any serious business environment. It is the essential quality in a manager that allows him or her to listen to criti-cism from subordinates (criticism which, by definition, always offers an alternative interpre-tation of events). It is the essential quality in the young associate attorney who prepares a client to testify by arguing the other side's position. And it is the central skill in any customer relations department.

Building Vocabulary

The Oxford English Dictionary lists over 500,000 words—excluding hundreds of thousands of technical terms—over twice the available vocabulary of either French or Ger-man, and the average native speaker knows only 50,000 of them, while using roughly 2,000 in the course of a week. Recent years have seen a rise in books and CD courses that offer to teach people "power words" that will help them in their professional lives. Companies like Verbal Advantage and Ultimate Vocabulary have prospered by marketing their educational materials to people who are concerned that their meager vocabularies will hold them back in their career paths.

English majors in every generation build their vocabularies by reading outside the normal vocabulary range of the contemporary mass media, which offer readers and viewers only a small percentage of the words available to them in books. I do not mean to suggest that being well schooled in the language of the English Renaissance and the jargon of post-modern literary criticism directly prepares students to succeed in business, but it does prepare students to be able to read and digest texts of tremendous difficulty in structure and syntax, and it accustoms them to the process of learning the specialized vocabulary of any discipline, whether it be that of law, information science, or environmental economics. Students who are comfortable reading both a Renaissance playwright like Shakespeare and a twentieth-century philosopher like Heidegger have already demonstrated the capacity to acquire vocabulary on their own through reading. This is not to say that the products of PowerVocabulary-Builder.com and Executive-Vocabulary.com are not helpful for English graduates; it is simply to say that for a trained English major, the purpose of increasing vocabulary has nothing to do with impressing people and everything to do with formulating ideas and expressing them appropriately to audiences of all kinds.

Strunk and White, in their classic book *Elements of Style* offered a simple piece of advice in writing style: "Do not be tempted by a twenty-dollar word when there is a ten-center handy, ready, and able." The authors, great lovers of language themselves, were not arguing against erudite language; they argued instead against using language in inappropriate ways. Certainly, in transactional writing, when a writer's purpose is to communicate ideas and information clearly and simply, choosing arcane vocabulary when common language is available reduces the chances that the idea will get across—worse yet, it does so for no constructive purpose.

Composition textbook writers have great fun with this issue of matching diction (word choice) to audience and situation. My point in raising this issue as a matter of literary study is that no writer can make an informed decision about options in word choice if his or her brain is not packed full of words to begin with. A writer with an internal thesaurus loaded up with a few hundred thousand English words will be better prepared to discern the language an audience needs than will a writer with no such verbal command.

The examinations that keep the gate before college (the ACT and SAT) and before graduate school (e.g. the GRE, GMAT) test students' vocabularies very openly. The idea is that a large and active vocabulary is an essential part of success in higher education at any level. English majors are expected to look at new words as they would their favorite food, whether those words be common terms or the discipline-specific jargon of any field. They are expected to take delight in their ability to express their ideas in a variety of tones by virtue of word choice alone, from the poetic language of aphorism ("Birds of a feather flock together") to the frozen prose of scientific reporting ("Members of associated aviary species congregate"). None of that flexibility as a writer is possible without first building a large and ever-growing vocabulary, not only in terms of the number of words, but also of the connotative meanings of individual words. As a colleague in creative writing recently pointed out to me, it *matters* whether we say "Mom," "Ma," "Mama," or "Mother."

An August 2007 Associated Press-Ipsos poll indicated that a quarter of Americans had not read one book in 2006. This was a much more literate result than the 2004 National Endowment of the Arts study that found only 57% of American adults had read a book in

2002. Add into the mix that the majority of reading is in popular fiction and biography, and we should not be surprised that Americans' vocabularies are generally limited to the words one encounters in the mass media. If it is true that America is increasingly becoming a "post-reading" culture, versed only in the language of electronic popular media, then it would follow that English majors do indeed have a "verbal advantage" in the real world of business, and that advantage stems from the many hours they spent reading literature and criticism that challenged their verbal status quo.

Growing as a Writer

With the emphasis in the literature classroom on learning how to think beyond the narrow confines of one's own experience and values, English majors necessarily grow as writers for a number of important reasons beyond the continual growth of an active vocabulary. They use writing as a means of discovering their own values and ideas; they use writing to uncover alternative interpretations that they could not have reached without entering into the long process of writing a paper; they discover in their research and class discussion how deeply varied the breadth of interpretation is across the varied groups of readers—feminist readers, Marxist readers, Freudian readers, readers from various religious backgrounds, readers from different cultural backgrounds. By thinking deeply for weeks about any given writing assignment, by engaging alternative close readings of the same text, by engaging multiple critical voices in their writing process, students of literature learn how to shape their own ideas amid a larger conversation of critical thought. They also learn to speak in the discipline-specific language of literary criticism, something many of them will do again when they move into an area of work that has its own jargon. Whether it be the law, hotel management, or nursing home administration, every industry has its own internal "language" that will need to be acquired and mastered.

The writing assignments that constitute most (and sometimes all) of the grading in literature classrooms challenge students to engage extraordinarily complicated topics in such areas as culture, ethics, philosophy, and psychology. Students then are required to test their own native point of view against the views of literary critics and theorists who have already written on the subject, as well as against the views of their classmates and professor as they showed themselves in discussion.

Very commonly, professors will limit the field of paper topics to a few general areas especially pertinent to the course design and require students to develop their own topics in the course of their research. Consequently, many of the topics English majors have engaged in recent years follow the trends in critical conversation since the 1980s. Students are asked to examine scholarly commentary in feminist criticism, psychological criticism, cultural criticism, etc., but their purpose in research is not simply to learn what other readers think about the texts at hand, but to discover what the students' own points of view really are. More importantly, they are required to test the validity of their own interpretations and the interpretations of others by learning not to assert points in their writing that are not backed up by a close examination of evidence.

The literary essays that English majors write are very disciplined exercises in critical thinking. They assert an original, overarching point of view on a complex issue, and then they defend that position with a logically structured examination of evidence taken from the text(s) at issue, as well as from the published arguments that preceded the student's interest. Thus, as English majors pore through the dense and challenging reading in literary theory and criticism, they grow as critical thinkers. Likewise, when someone chooses to hire an English major—as opposed to a more "applied" major in a specific area of business—that employer has chosen to hire a thinker, and better yet, a thinker who can write.

Examining Literary "Canons," Partaking in Shared Culture

To the great horror of many in recent years, Shakespeare has been removed as a requirement in many English programs around the country. Alarmed by this trend, the American Council of Trustees and Alumni commissioned and issued a study on the phenomenon titled *The Vanishing Shakespeare* (http://www.goacta.org/publications/ Reports/Vanishing-Shakespeare.pdf). Their group looked at seventy major colleges and universities—including the Ivy League and Seven Sisters, the Big 10 universities, the *U.S. News and World Report* top 25 national universities and liberal arts colleges, select public universities in California and New York, and all the English departments in the Washington D.C. area. What they found is that Shakespeare is required in only 15 of the 70 schools, or 21%. Only one of the eight Ivy-League schools, Harvard, still had a Shakespeare requirement at the time of the April 2007 study.

Typically, those who are horrified by the widespread disappearance of required courses in Shakespeare hold to the traditional view advanced in the 18th century by Dr. Samuel Johnson and in the 19th century by Matthew Arnold 1) that "great books" offer aesthetic, civic, and moral instruction to readers, 2) that we know great books because they continue to instruct and edify people throughout the centuries, and 3) that great books, and the authors who wrote them, can be taught and must be taught as a "canon" of works that help a society define and understand itself. In addition, they embrace Samuel Taylor Coleridge's assessment of Shakespeare as "The Great Bard." Before Coleridge's work popularized him, Shakespeare had been considered just one among many fine English playwrights, and first Chaucer and later Milton were considered the towering giants of literature that everyone needed to know.

E.D. Hirsch presented a defense of such a case adamantly in his 1987 blockbuster *Cultural Literacy: What Every American Needs to Know*, in which he argued that in order to communicate effectively in civic discourse, American citizens need to have a shared body of knowledge that serves as contextual background in their communications. In the late 1990s, Hirsch went on to publish his "Core Knowledge Series," in which he suggests what knowledge young people need to acquire and at what stage of their education. Hirsch argues that a focus on critical-thinking skills, without attention to the literature being examined, is wrong-headed. In the wake of Hirsch's work, a small publishing boom took off in the area of cultural literacy, including dictionaries and encyclopedias that purport to identify specifically those things that all Americans should know.

One problem with any argument for a canon of literature that everyone needs to know is that it is simply impossible to cover all of the great works by the great writers in the English language in the dozen or so courses required in a typical English major curriculum. The notion of "coverage" is at all times a mirage. Practically speaking, the canon of works that everyone should know was loosely accepted as those authors and works included in the literary anthologies that made the teaching of "survey" courses possible.

In the curricular reform at many colleges that has removed Shakespeare as a requirement for *all* English majors, no one has argued that Shakespeare is not the most widely read and influential writer in the English tradition (this is a statistical fact); no one has argued that Shakespeare is unimportant or that his works should not be taught. What was argued is that Shakespeare's influence in literary history, as well as in world culture, should not privilege Shakespeare Studies over all the other important divisions of literatures in English as the sole author to be *required* as a universal course requirement. In response, the conservative American Council of Trustees and Alumni posed the question, "If Shakespeare is not central to a liberal education, what is?" They in fact go further to encourage the major financial contributors to the colleges in question to pressure university administrators for curricular change in English that would focus on "major authors."

The tension behind this disagreement in many ways comes down to different premises about the fundamental purpose of literary study. On one side we have the idea that the ultimate good of English education is a set of transferable skills; on the other is the idea that the ultimate good of English education is a body of knowledge that allows one to communicate in civil society. The happy reality, however, is that both positions are true; better yet, these positions are in no way mutually exclusive.

One does not have to embrace a narrow canon of "great books" in order to see that there is such a thing as excellence in literary achievement. Contemporary canon revisionists are not out to eliminate the knowledge of Shakespeare, Milton, and Chaucer. Instead, they have struggled to add new writers and new works that expand the canon to include great writers ignored in past models (often women and people of color) and to include contemporary writers whose works are yet to pass the test of time that inevitably identifies literature as "influential," "classic," or otherwise worthy to be taught.

Contemporary English majors still read canonical works (Shakespeare included) in virtually all of their lower-level literature courses, and the vast majority of course offerings nationwide still focus mainly on the literature of writers who have generated a long bibliography of critical writing that by its very existence testifies to some level of cultural importance. They come away from their literature courses with a solid body of knowledge in American literature, often including significant reading in African-American and Native-American writers, knowledge that earlier generations typically did not have. They come away with knowledge of Chaucer, Milton, Wordsworth, Arnold, and Pound, but in addition to that they have knowledge of post-colonial writers in Africa, Australia, India, and Latin and South America.

Although we might well agree with the argument that a shared body of literary reading will give citizens a useful means of connecting with one another and thinking through important issues in society, we also have to acknowledge that the canon of literature worthy of literary analysis is far, far too large to simply say, "We all need to read books A, B, and C, and not books D, E, and F."

When English majors graduate, they are merely beginning their lives as adult readers. If our English programs have had their desired effect, our graduates will be reading and discussing the ever-expanding canon of great literature for the rest of their lives. They will be supporting living writers, attending the dramatic productions of new playwrights and screenwriters. They will subscribe to the journals that publish short stories, poetry, and essays that will ultimately produce the next generation of "great books." And they will encourage their communities to share that literary wealth with them in book clubs, in library programs, and in their communities' schools.

No such civic development will be possible, of course, unless we graduate English majors with the skills they need to thrive in the careers of their choice, and it *is* their skills, and not their knowledge of Shakespeare specifically, that will allow for that success.

CHAPTER 4:

Composition—Writing for Diverse Audiences

The Universal Nature of Composition Instruction

Although "composition" is taught in different ways at different colleges and universities, virtually everyone agrees that the ability to write is a basic skill that all college students need help developing. Thus, almost all entering freshmen have some sort of required course in composition. Whether it be called "composition," "rhetoric," or "English," these courses focus on training students in a set of skills fairly universal across the colleges. These courses are designed to help students succeed not only with the writing that will be required of them in academic settings, but also in their careers after college. Thus freshman composition courses typically share the following key objectives:

- To help students communicate clearly with specific audiences in specific situations;
- To help students become competent in grammar, punctuation, and mechanics;
- To help students master all aspects of the process of writing;
- To help students document the sources they incorporate in their writing.

Students will find these basics objectives worded in different ways, but freshman composition is one of the easiest courses to transfer between schools because the objectives, and even the methods, are so similar college to college. Some schools require only three semester hours, some four, some six, but everyone has a requirement.

Typically, composition courses are the only place where non-English majors actually get any *training* in writing whatsoever—whether it be in focused principles of grammar and sentence structure or in the larger areas of paragraph and essay structure. Students may write a great deal in the many disciplines of the academy, but their non-English faculty will rarely take the time to mark or to explain the problems they see in the writing, nor do they typically suggest ways of fixing those problems. Many do not feel competent themselves to instruct students in such ways; others simply see that work as the responsibility of the English department alone. Grading essays for course content is difficult enough for non-English faculty; grading for writing, too, would take an enormous amount of time, and therefore it rarely happens outside the English classroom. This is why English majors—who receive a great deal of individualized writing instruction, as opposed to one or two courses—bring an unusually high level of writing expertise into the workplace.

Common Misconceptions about Composition

Although at some point, all college graduates take or test out of freshman composition, many people remember very little of their own composition training over time, and we in the discipline of English wind up hearing all sorts of myths that shock us.

1. Grammar is Everything

This first widespread idea is surprisingly common. People assume that a composition course will focus almost entirely on issues of "correct" grammar, or more broadly on notions of correct usage and punctuation. Few misconceptions could be more wrong. Again, decades of research in grammar studies, have gone to show that students simply do not increase their grammatical skills when principles of grammar are taught in a void, outside the context of students' actual writing. This is not to say that grammar is not important, but that for students actually to grow in their command of grammar, they need to write a great deal and to learn from their own individual set of mistakes, over and over and over.

In composition courses, grammar is seldom, if ever, an issue of in-class discussion. It is taught in highly individualized ways to each student. If some one grammatical issue appears in the majority of papers for one assignment, the instructor might devote some time to that issue, but that would be in the context of writing, not grammar instruction for its own sake. Much of that instruction also occurs in one-on-one conferences between professor and student, as well as in the one-on-one tutorial services offered by college and university writing centers around the country.

Grammar is indeed taught, but it is seldom a large factor in the evaluation of writing in college. It will much more often affect a grade as a minor percentage of the total assessment. Much more important in a composition class is the clarity, coherence, and completeness of a paper's overall argument. To make too big a deal out of grammatical issues would be to diminish the larger, much more important issues of critical thought and the persuasive analysis of evidence. Grammar is simply one element in the larger whole of effective writing.

2. The Standards of Good Writing are Universal

This idea is much more controversial than the first common misunderstanding. Part of the problem is semantic. It *is* universally true that the audience and situation determine the effectiveness of any standard of good writing, and so one could argue that there is a universal standard. But when people argue for "Standards of English," they are typically trying to advance an agenda that one type of writing style should be seen as always and everywhere superior to another, or that grammatical and stylistic "rules" are never to be broken. Such arguments typically begin with the words "You can never":

- "You can never start as sentence with a coordinating conjunction."
- "You can never split an infinitive."
- "You can't end a sentence with a preposition."

None of these "universal" rules has ever been true, of course. Chaucer and Shakespeare began beautiful sentences with coordinating conjunctions (and, or, for, but, nor, so, yet), as have renowned writers throughout the ages since. Writers split their infinitives whenever placing the adverb somewhere else in the sentence proves to be somehow less effective. For instance, Captain Kirk, in the first *Star Trek* series, declared that the starship Enterprise's mission was "to *boldly* go where no man has gone before," not "to go boldly where no man has gone before" or "to go where no man has gone before . . . boldly." And Winston Churchill is credited with the following memorable sentence: "A preposition is a marvelous thing to end a sentence with."

    A secure and educated writer is not bound by pre-determined "universal" rules. We are all, however, bound by those rules determined by our actual audiences in the actual situations in which we write, and those audiences and situations more often than not embrace common standards both in grammar and in word choice. The challenge before the student of composition is not how to apply standards of usage on any audience; the challenge is how to determine which standards apply to the audience at hand.

    What I ask of students is that they split their infinitives *on purpose*, after they have consciously decided that the adverb works best in that position. So, too, I expect them to offend their audience on purpose, not because they were unaware that many of their readers would be offended. For instance, many readers are put off by the masculine pronoun reference to an indefinite-singular subject (e.g. "If a doctor makes a mistake, he is in danger of a malpractice suit"); others find the use of the feminine both smug and distracting ("If a doctor makes a mistake, she is in danger of a malpractice suit). Both choices can be damaging to a writer's relationship to the audience, and so most style handbooks encourage student writers to learn to avoid the use of the indefinite singular unless it is somehow vital to use it ("If doctors make mistakes, they are in danger of a malpractice suit"). Everyone draws a line at some point at which they stop caring about an audience's sensibility. "Waitperson" and "personhole" are not universally accepted language, by any means. Writers always have to judge the appropriateness of their choices against the nature of the audience.

3. One Writing Course is All It Takes

    I took college math for two full years in college, and by the time I completed my course in differential equations, I was thinking in math for the first time in my life. Now, nearly thirty years later, I could not "integrate by parts" if my life depended on it. So it is with composition. If a student takes a freshman composition course and then does not write regularly for the next year, the skills gained in that course will very likely be lost. I am functioning adequately without the advanced mathematical skills of my youth, but the skills that we develop in composition are essential throughout one's working life, regardless the nature of one's career.

Freshman composition is a small first step in developing writing skills, and as English has developed over the past twenty years, more and more courses in advanced composition have entered the curriculum. Washington University in St. Louis speaks to the importance of such course offerings in the "Career Opportunities" section of their Department Website, and their point applies no matter what college or university an English major chooses to attend:

> Students who plan careers in law, business, or publishing would do well to include courses in advanced composition; writing and communications skills are essential in these areas and should be developed as fully as possible. Courses in literary criticism should not be scanted, however.

Key Goals of Composition Instruction

Over the years, the field of Composition Studies has been remarkably consistent in it primary goals, although the methods by which we in the profession of English try to accomplish those goals develops constantly. The National Council for the Teaching of English has been defining goals, promoting research, and setting educational policy in the way that writing is taught in America since 1911. In 2004, the "Writing Study Group" of the Executive Committee issued a document entitled *NCTE Beliefs about the Teaching of Writing*. This document lays out a series of common beliefs that underpin the goals and purposes of writing instruction, a few of which are summarized below:

- Everyone can become a better writer.
- Students learn to write by writing.
- Writing is a process.
- Writing is a tool for thinking.
- Writing serves and proceeds from many purposes.
- Conventions in format and editing matter.
- Writing and reading are related.
- Writing happens in the midst of complex social relationships.

When I was young, English majors heard simliar truisms like "Writing is about the three C's: clarity, clarity, clarity!" or "Writing is about the three C's: clarity, coherence, and completeness!" or "Writing is revision!" And indeed there is great truth in all three clichéd statements. In Composition Studies today, however, people generally steer clear of sweeping generalizations with the understanding that what makes writing effective, what makes clarity *possible* varies as the audiences and situations of the documents vary. Increasingly, we see an emphasis on the importance of understanding a targeted audience and adapting the message to the perceived needs of that audience.

In addition to the emphasis on matching the message to the audience and situation, contemporary composition courses stress the incorporation of images, charts, and graphs, as the texts in modern society become increasingly electronic in their delivery. Of particular importance, then, to the 70% of English majors who will go on to careers in business and public service are those course offerings in Business and Technical Writing, in which visual rhetoric and the adaptation of message to audience is primary, as opposed to composition courses in expository or persuasive writing that emphasize more narrowly the formulation and expression of ideas in complex arenas of thought.

Business and Technical Writing

English Departments now routinely offer upper-level courses with titles like "Business Writing," "Technical Writing," "Writing in the Professions," and "Business Communications." These courses, like all composition courses, teach writing as a process; they teach writing as a social transaction; they teach critical thought and logical processes; they help students make progress in their editing skills. But these courses also stress the importance of matching a message to the wide variety of audiences that exist in the working world: expert audiences, lay audiences, technical audiences, disinterested audiences, uneducated audiences, angry audiences, or foreign audiences, to identify only a few. Much more so than a course in freshman composition—which typically assumes an academic audience—a business-writing course will involve a series of audience and situational analyses that force the writer to consider how a message will need to be organized and delivered with consideration to the audience's need for visual aids, for brevity, and for clarity.

Writing from Models

Courses in professional writing are commonly structured around the types of writing situations common to the world of work. Courses in business communications and technical writing naturally have a great deal of overlap because technical writing inevitably occurs in some kind of business environment. Whether a person works as a mechanical engineer or as a financial office in a bank, he or she will be required to write business letters and memos, progress reports, proposals. However, the more technically oriented professions have special needs in their reporting—in the presentation of technical data, in the presentation of mechanical processes, technical instructions, and mechanism description. In retail business, banking, and securities, on the other hand, more will be demanded in the area of customer communications, requiring training in various types of letters (sales letters, adjustment letters, interoffice memos) and in the conventions of communication within the various industries.

Given a textbook model of a progress report, for instance, complete with a detailed explanation of each structural element of the report, students might be assigned the task of writing an original progress report on some aspect of their off-campus work or summer internships. Students might read and analyze five different types of proposal reports and then be assigned a project in which they write a proposal that 1) identifies a real problem or need on campus or in a workplace and 2) suggests a strategy that will help solve that problem or fulfill that need. The key here is that students learn a set of writing conventions and forms that they then are able to adapt to a variety of workplace situations.

In response to the diverse nature of the professional writing needs of the workplace, English departments have developed discrete courses that offer students solid models of professional communications and then ask the students to use the models to frame original letters, reports, and proposals. These courses are so popular around the country that the text-book industry in this area has thrived, and the books themselves serve as excellent desktop reference manuals for students as they move into writing-intensive lines of work. The skills these courses impart are also so clearly valued by industry that Ph.D.-granting institutions have trouble persuading their graduates to go into lower-paying academic positions rather than accept the much more lucrative offers that Ph.D.'s in Professional Writing command in the open market.

Balancing Conciseness and Completeness

Along with the structural models that professional-writing courses give students, they also impose a special emphasis on conciseness, the idea that in workplace reporting espe-cially, a professional writer has to communicate all the necessary information the audience needs in the fewest words necessary. This is, for good or ill, not the norm in other modes of writing. Traditional essay writing, for instance, rarely advocates the liberal use of headings or the incorporation of photos, drawings, and diagrams. In creative non-fiction, the use of rich, esoteric word choices can be a great virtue, in that the audience can be assumed to share in the writer's accelerated love of language. But in business, where time is money and where the essential purpose is the transmittal of information, conciseness is a self-defined virtue.

Therefore, in the world of professional writing, the national anthem would need to be rewritten: "Is the flag that we saw last night during the battle still visible this morning?" So too, the content of Shakespeare's beloved 14-line sonnet "Let us not to the marriage of true minds admit impediments" would be much more direct: "I think that love that changes isn't really love." And the 23rd Psalm would merit some revision, especially from the melliflu-ous King James version of the Bible: "God takes care of me like a shepherd does his sheep, so I am not afraid of things." The world is fortunately a richer and happier place in that the "rules" that govern professional reporting are by no means the "universal standard rules of English."

Against, then, the business world's need for conciseness, there is the crosscurrent need for completeness. Any document that does not communicate to the audience *everything* that audience needs is, by definition, *too* concise. Professional writing must be simultane-ously concise and complete. In order to pursue that balanced goal, textbooks in this area supply real-world examples of reports that are too wordy, as exercises in revision for concise-ness, and they also offer examples of reports that fall short of the audience's needs and ask students to identify those audience needs and to rewrite the report accordingly. Finding that balancing point for each document, with each unique audience, is never easy.

The Genuine Importance of Grammar

As I have already said repeatedly, little is more misunderstood about English than the role that grammar plays in our classroom practice. Everyone in America grows up learning grammar in teaching units that focus on the parts of speech (noun, preposition, adverb, etc.) and how those parts of speech relate to one another. As we grow up, grammar concepts are taught on their own, outside the context of writing, in a series of auto-graded quizzes and tests that impose a long series of punishments on students who take too long to learn pronoun case or the nature of the past-participial phrase. And all over America, everywhere I go, people remember their experience of junior-high and high-school English with anxiety.

Along with that reality, then, we have the simple fact that decades of research by Ph.D.s in English and linguistics has almost universally declared that isolated grammar instruction does not improve writing. This is not to say that students do not need to learn grammar or that English teachers should not teach grammar. What it does mean, though, is that our traditional methods have not been as effective as they could be.

English majors, in order to excel at the craft, have to develop a deep-seated, genuine love of language in all its amazing complexity. Without an authentic love of language, no one will ever go through the long and painful process of learning from our own mistakes with the grammar we are slow to acquire. Without a solid command of grammar, mid-level managers are not going to be able to explain to their superiors *why* a clause in a contract does not express what it is meant to express. Without knowing grammar, professional correspondence and professional reporting will be unclear, ambiguous, and impenetrable in all sorts of needless ways.

If anyone doubts the necessity of learning the grammatical structures of our language, all we have to do is look at the documents of government. The relationships of word groups one to another are typically so cluttered, cumbersome, and unclear that on June 1, 1998, President Clinton issued a *Memorandum on Plain Language in Government* (http://www. plainlanguage.gov/whatisPL/govmandates/memo.cfm), which ordered government workers to pursue the following goals in their writing:

- Logical organization
- Easy-to-read design features
- Common, everyday words, except for necessary technical words
- "You" and other pronouns
- Short sentences.

In spite of high-court rulings like the U.S. 9th Circuit's *Walters v. Reno*—which argued that the Immigration and Naturalization Service's deportation documents were so unreadable as to violate deportees' due-process rights—much of the government documents Americans encounter in their lives (medical privacy statements, IRS tax instructions, etc.) remain highly unreadable even by the most educated Americans.

In over twenty years of teaching college English, I have identified a finite list of grammatical issues that trouble college-educated people. For the most part, for instance, they understand conceptually the four basic functions of the comma:

1. to offset introductory elements
2. to separate series items in a list
3. to separate independent clauses connected by a coordinating conjunction
4. to offset parenthetical elements.

But knowing the theoretical concepts is not enough. If a writer cannot recognize a coordinating conjunction (and, or, for, but, nor, so, yet) then rule number 3 is rendered inoperative. Rule 3 is also useless if the writer cannot judge whether a group of words is a clause or not. It is also useless if the writer cannot judge is the clause is independent or not.

Likewise, a writer will be a poor judge of whether or not an adjective clause is parenthetical or not if that person cannot recognize a group of words as an adjective clause in the first place (e.g. "Let's start at the very beginning, <u>which is a very good place to start</u>."). Furthermore, not all introductory commas are optional. My favorite example of this point can be found in the *Harbrace College Handbook*: "Still water is good for you." If the writer drops the comma after "Still," the sentence means something hilariously untrue. Still, stagnant water grows mono-cellular organisms that will turn your tonsils green. The difficult task with introductory commas is to get past what you *mean* and to see what you have actually *written* in terms of what the audience will understand.

Another common grammatical problem, more large-scale than punctuation, is that writers struggle with the concept of "parallelism" when they do not know the more complex parts of speech (e.g. noun clauses, gerund phrases, infinitive phrases, participial phrases). Parallelism is a wonderfully orderly aspect of language. It arises naturally in the development of every language on earth, without ever being instituted by a squad of grammar police. The issue here is that when we put groups of words in series, every element in series needs to be grammatically equal: "Joe likes that you arrive on time, that you are able to work with little supervision, and your ability to form friendships with your co-workers." Three things are brought in parallel here, two noun clauses and a noun phrase. The verb can operate on each element in series, but when the three parts are read sequentially, we encounter a grammatical train wreck. Cognitive linguists see parallelism not simply as a grammatical rule but as a fundamental construct of the human mind. Analogy and metaphor also work this way: the things we compare must be fundamentally similar structures in order for the comparison to make sense. The same is true for parables, as well. When our parallel structures break down, grammar clearly matters.

Other types of grammatical difficulty become downright embarrassing in the real world of work. One of the most obvious areas is the touchy subject of pronoun case—when one uses "I," for instance, and when "me." A manager who is not in command of pronoun case risks losing credibility in the eyes of clients: "Me and my team would like to propose a new approach to you logistical problems." And though most style manuals now accept that writers can simply begin sentences with "Who," regardless of the ultimate case of the pronoun, we commonly expect someone to use "whom" when the pronoun is clearly the object of a verb or preposition: "To who should I address this?" "To who" sounds like a British hunting cry or a bird call, and it demonstrates that there are in fact limits to the flexibility of grammatical norms.

A working and ever-growing knowledge of grammar is an essential part of any thinking life. English majors, like their fellow foreign-language majors, have a privileged opportunity to become more expert in the ways in which their language operates than any other major on a college campus. It allows for the close readings in literary study, and it allows English majors to see exactly why different groups of readers can read the same text so differently. Take the Second Commandment, for instance. Adherents of Judaism and Islam read the text one way, and Christians read it another. The difference has everything to do with how we see the grammatical structures operating (regardless the language of the translation from the Ancient Hebrew):

> I am the Lord your God, who brought you out of the land of Egypt, out of the house of slavery; you shall have no other gods before me. You shall not make for yourself an idol, whether in the form of anything that is in heaven above, or that is on the earth beneath, or that is in the water under the earth. You shall not bow down to them or worship them.

In the Jewish tradition, and likewise in the Islamic, each individual clause is interpreted as a binding command:

> Part A: "You shall have no other gods before me."
> Part B: "You shall not make for yourself an idol . . ."
> Part C: "You shall not bow down to them or worship them"

In these two world religions, part B is understood to forbid the production of any representative art, with the assumption that art that takes "form" from anything in air, earth, or water is to be understood as potentially idolatrous. Consequently, Jewish and Islamic art and architecture are historically non-representational, ornate in design but not in image.

Christian tradition essentially reduced the entire multi-clause commandment into "Because I am your one true God, you will not construct or worship false idols." Thus the Christian tradition of the West is marked with centuries of representative art—not of other Gods (idols) that they worship ahead of or alongside the Trinity, but of things material (nature, the bodies of saints, etc.) and things of the heavens (angels, the Holy Spirit, God the Father, etc.). This is an amazingly significant interpretive difference, and like all such divergent interpretations, it is grounded in alternative views on the relationship of one group of words to the next, as well as on differing understandings of the word "idol" in this context.

Collaborative Writing

Children in elementary and middle school are now accustomed to "group projects," assignments in virtually any class that require them to meet after school and go through a series of unavoidable preliminary tasks: forming teams, setting goals, assigning tasks, researching the topics, negotiating with and getting to know one another. Once the individual assignments are in place, the schoolchildren then attempt to go through the standard early elements of a writing process—planning, brainstorming, outlining, drafting, revising—only to reassemble and add a key element that single-author writing does not entail: the attempt to build consensus. Once the contentious process of consensus-building is complete, the student team then moves on to the finalizing tasks of editing, proofreading, layout, and delivery (typically a paper with an accompanying poster presentation of some kind).

What schoolchildren everywhere discover early in their lives is that collaborative writing can be very frustrating. They find that teammates can be uncooperative or overbearing; they find that building consensus can be difficult or impossible; and they find that some methods of dividing labor are better than others; and they learn that the division of labor is often highly inequitable. None of those areas of frustration change when collaborative writing occurs in the workplace, and so English majors are wise to seek out classroom training in this area.

English research into collaborative writing has made tremendous strides in the last twenty years, with the result that instruction in team writing projects is more informed and much more systematic than it was in the past. Classroom practice now includes writing assignments that focus on specific aspects of collaboration:

- Team formation (what role each member plays—writer, consultant, facilitator, team leader, researcher, technical analyst, etc.)
- Process and division of labor (who does what when)
- Team communications (how the team members cooperate along the process)
- Technology (what software products the team can use and to what effect).

This last element will come as a surprise to many, but given that in industries of all kinds, collaborative writing projects pull together people in different offices, often in different buildings, corporate and academic IT specialists have developed a wide variety of electronic tools to make collaborative writing easier and more efficient.

"Groupware," something also referred to "Collaborative Software," is a group of products developed to serve the professional needs of everyone involved in collaborative writing. Lotus Notes was one of the first products in this area, and the standard electronic functions of e-mail and text messaging have also supported collaborative writing, but now there are comprehensive software programs competing with each other to develop new and more efficient means of supporting collaborative writing projects. Such software programs allow for writers at remote sites to brainstorm together, to reach consensus by discussion or by vote, and to share images, text documents, and spreadsheets. These programs are not necessarily known by all employers, and they are not self-explanatory, but instead require significant training in order to serve their purpose. Thus, an English major trained in both the processes and the technologies of collaborative writing has an immensely useful skill to share with an employer.

Visual Rhetoric

In courses in professional writing, language constitutes only one part of the overall subject of study. Often a message is made immensely more clear not by words but by the judicious use of horizontal and vertical white space; by the inclusion of pictures, drawings, charts, graphs, and tables; or by the manipulation of font type, point size, boldface, italics, colors, bullets, or numbers. Again, these elements of presentation are referred to as "visual rhetoric" in the discipline of English. Visual rhetoric is an essential element of almost all professional writing, allowing the writer to communicate efficiently and effectively what might be nearly impossible with words alone. By no means is it the domain of English alone; to the contrary, we in English look for guidance to our colleagues in Media Studies, in Graphic Design, in Marketing and in Public Relations, in Computer and Business Information Systems, in Civil and Mechanical Engineering. All of these disciplines require their students to learn the software programs native to their related professions. Some programs offer courses that teach students to use such tools as AutoCAD (Computer Aided Design), Adobe Photoshop, Excel, Microsoft Project, and all of the programs require their students to write documents that integrate text with the visual aids.

In the English side of this shared mission to graduate students with expertise in professional communication, our Professional Writing courses require students to produce Marketing and PR materials (newsletters, tri-fold brochures) and illustrated reports of all kinds (proposal reports, research reports, progress reports, consulting reports). Many English classrooms do not go beyond the visual-rhetoric capabilities of Microsoft Word or WordPerfect (both of which have excellent internal capabilities), but students who already have skills in other software packages are encouraged to apply those skills while crafting their documents and to share with their classmates the special advantages of that particular tool or set of tools. Such exchange of ideas is possible because upper-level courses in Professional Writing (Business or Technical) are typically open to all majors, and English majors are exposed to the unique demands of writing in such fields as Industrial Engineering, Finance, Communications, or Environmental Studies. The exact software tools may vary, the technical jargon may vary, but the writing process, the importance of audience analysis, and the need for visual rhetoric remain the same.

In all its diverse sub-elements, Composition Studies can play an important role in an English major's development as a future business leader. It reinforces the overarching principle in English that the audience and the situation of a piece of writing determine what can or cannot be done in constructing the document—whether it be a matter of vocabulary, or of style, or of the extent to which the information and ideas are organized, expressed, or amplified by visual aids. English is always a social enterprise, and a good writer knows the needs of the audience and writes with those needs in mind.

CHAPTER 5:
Creative Writing—
Making Something Out of Nothing

Each year, the *Harvard Business Review* issues its "Breakthrough Ideas" issue to highlight issues and ideas that drove change in the business world in any given year. In the 2004 issue, one of the articles meant to inspire and challenge managers was Daniel Pink's article "The MFA is the New MBA." Pink begins by pointing out that while Harvard's M.B.A. program admitted 10% of its applicants, the UCLA graduate school in the Fine Arts admitted only 3% of its own applicants. He goes on to say that "With applications climbing and ever more arts grads occupying key corporate positions, the master of fine arts is becoming the new business degree." Pink recognized that in 2004, more and more major companies were realizing that they could gain a competitive edge in their markets by making their products "transcendent—physically beautiful and emotionally compelling," citing the aesthetic appeal of the iMac computer and the nationwide artistic redesign of the Target Corporation's store aisles.

Pink's call in *HBR* led to speculation among university leaders as to whether they might try to create a graduate *business* degree program that would focus on the creative arts, something that might be called an "Executive M.F.A." Such programs would focus on creativity, the idea being that America's business leaders could use the academy's help developing their innate creative abilities. Such a call acknowledges that businesses are led forward by visionary people who can imagine what is not yet there, those people who can think innovatively, not just to invent new products or new services, but to imagine new ways to make old things work better or more efficiently. They acknowledged that a ledger's bottom line is often advanced the most by the creative imagination of a company's leaders.

This leads inevitably to the issue of whether or not creativity can be taught in the first place, and I am certainly not in any position to settle that longstanding debate. I can say, however, that creativity is nurtured, encouraged, challenged, and exercised in the creative writing programs in hundreds of English departments all over the country. We cannot say that coursework in creative writing will necessarily increase a person's general level of creativity, but we can say that this particular division of English Studies leads people to reach into their imaginations and create works of fiction, poetry, drama out of the blank page. Standard courses in composition and literature negotiate ideas within a community of thinkers; creative writing, on the other hand, encounters and recreates the world in art, and thus if it does not actually *teach* people to be more creative, it presents the students with a means to uncover the creativity that was already there inside.

In the discipline of Creative Writing, students find their creativity in the things in front of them. It might be an experience visiting a grandparent in a nursing home; it might be an experience in a check-out lane; it might be a story in the newspaper or on the student's computer homepage in the morning. Creative Writing faculty lead students to the creative act by having them work within forms of all kinds. In addition to presenting multiple examples, the faculty offer the students guidelines, a frame in which to generate the student's own original vision. For prose, the fundamental unit will be the sentence; for poetry it will be the line. They might be asked to write a work of literature about a work of work of art. They might be asked to write a sonnet or a narrative poem. They might be asked to write about a political issue. But when they sit down in a quiet place to work, no matter what the guidelines may be, a creative-writing student has to create something out of nothing. They have to exercise their imaginative capacity to *invent*.

Fostering Creativity

In order to see how creative writing achieves its goals as creative art, one has to understand the unique methodology of the workshop method of instruction. Most of the credit for the development of this method goes back to the origins of the Iowa Writer's Workshop. In 1922, innovative thinkers at the University of Iowa began to accept creative writing for graduate credit. Fourteen years later, they launched the Iowa Writer's Workshop under the direction of Wilbur Schramm. From its earliest beginnings, the Iowa program brought in some of the most accomplished writers in the English language to meet with their creative writing students, including John Berryman, Robert Lowell, Robert Frost, and Robert Penn Warren.

The method that comes down to us from those days is a classroom with 14-18 students and one faculty member, all sitting in a large circle as a community of creative artists. Such a course is self-selecting for students who want to try their hand at creative writing, which presupposes that they are all bound together, at the very least, in a shared love of literature as *art*. Rather than being bound together like most English majors, primarily as a community of thinkers, creative writing students bond as a cooperative team of artists, and those relationships run especially deep.

In a writing workshop setting, the instructor will assign a topic to the entire class, and the students then bring the completed assignments to class with a copy for each classmate, plus one for the teacher. Once all the papers are distributed, the students take the creative writing home, read through it all, and write down comments of praise and constructive suggestions for change. When the class reassembles, they begin a systematic process of critiquing each piece, one at a time. Some pieces draw little group critique, some draw a great deal, and in that process of group critique and discernment, important things happen beyond the actual literary art that the students produce. The students develop skills in giving and accepting criticism that allow them to set their egos aside and focus entirely on the literature at hand.

The communal, "teamwork" nature of creative writing as a discipline originates not simply from the Iowa Writer's Workshop; instead, the workshop model itself proceeded from something common in the history of literature. Like-minded groups of writers have always "schooled" together, read and critiqued one another, and helped one another reach their audiences. Sometimes the collaboration happened between a small group like the early Romantic writers William Wordsworth, Dorothy Wordsworth, and Samuel Taylor Coleridge or the later group of Percy Shelley, Mary Shelley, and Lord Byron. Sometimes the groups have been larger, and interdisciplinary, like the "Bloomsbury Group" of London in the early 20th century, a society of more than a dozen writers, artists, and intellectuals that included the novelist Virginia Woolf, the economist John Maynard Keynes, and the artist Duncan Grant. Likewise, Gertrude Stein gathered a society of writers and artists to herself in her home in the Montparnasse neighborhood of Paris between 1903 and the beginning of WWI. The same thing occurred with the Beat Generation that first gathered in the 1940s with the young Jack Kerouac, Allen Ginsberg, Neal Cassaday, and William S. Burroughs and then expanded to include such writers as the poets Gary Snyder and Lawrence Ferlinghetti. Because of their bonds of friendship, all these artists were able to *challenge* one another and to spur one another on to create revolutionary achievements in their various media. Creativity rarely advances in a vacuum, and the academic discipline of creative writing reflects this in the social fabric of its classroom methodology.

Group Dynamics in Creative Writing

Giving and Receiving Criticism

When creative writing students come to their first classroom experience, they typically do not believe that they have any personal experience worth writing about, and they need their faculty to convince them that the life they have lived is fertile ground for the discovery of art. Once the students begin to express things that matter deeply to them at some level, the process of class-wide critique become dangerous. Students lay themselves bare to one another; they make themselves extraordinarily vulnerable to personal hurt. My colleague, the poet Lee Newton, explains that in the early days of a creative writer's coursework, students tend to offer only praise—perhaps because they are not ready to offer the kind of negative criticism that they themselves are afraid to receive. Thus, he asks directive questions that bring what he calls the "broken" elements of the writing to the surface—issues of tone, metaphor, believability, naturalness of voice, economy of language, sound, etc.—so that the individual and the group can actually *learn* something from one another. In some cases my colleague also draws attention not to an identifiable problem, but to a "missed opportunity."

Without looking at what can be fixed, what can be improved, no real learning can take place. No one *likes* to hear about those things in their fiction, poetry, drama, and screenplays that others see as "broken," but any writer who wants to grow absolutely must learn how to cope with criticism—sometimes very blunt and harsh criticism—about things in their writing that are deeply personal, about scenes and characters and fictional events that they considered to be their very best work. Sometimes the remark can be both blunt and adolescent, "This sounds like a Hallmark card"; at other times is can be mean-spirited—"Were you high when you wrote this?" But my colleagues tell me that the person who does the critiquing can never really know when a criticism will hurt the feelings of the one being critiqued. What they do know is that the critiquing process is inevitably painful, but that by the time students are well into the program, they learn to separate the criticism of the work from criticism of the self, eventually becoming writers who are not only open to criticism but who actively seek it out.

That ability to accept painful criticism—without taking that criticism personally and without demonizing the messenger—is a business skill. So, too, is the ability to give constructive, fraternal criticism to someone, knowing that the criticism has the potential to hurt that person emotionally. These two linked skills deserve a word of their own, but our language cannot yet accommodate that need. "Ego strength," "diplomacy," and "sensitivity" are related terms, but they do not come close to expressing this important quality in a mature, professional approach to the workplace. Some of us will remember a line-item on grade school report cards that read "ability to accept criticism." As a nation, we know this quality is vital in child development, but somehow we stop talking about it as a unique skill when students grow up. In the creative writing classroom, this quality is a daily reality; it is, effectively, the principle mode of learning.

By the time creative writing students have completed two full courses together, virtually everyone has grown the "thick skin" that is required, that ability to place the ego aside somehow and to focus on the artistic issue itself, without personal rancor. Growth as a writer always requires this skill, in any mode of writing, but in creative writing, the personal stakes are by far the highest. In some cases, a young person may believe that his or her skill as a creative writer is at the very center of that person's self worth, and criticism of the writing is received entirely as criticism of the person. Such students either drop out of their first class, or they grow—not only in their skills as writers, but in the general self-confidence that is required for any modicum of personal happiness.

Creative writers everywhere are only able to accomplish this growth in accepting and giving criticism because they first build collegial relationships with their classmates, even the ones with whom they would not naturally share what the sociologist Max Weber termed "co-mensality," the willingness to sit together at a table and share a meal. Not all teammates like each other, but over time they come at least to respect one another enough to work together and learn from one another.

Writing as a Member of a Team

The creative writing workshop is like any group in which a team of people suffers together the pains of disciplined growth in a craft. Any high-school football player who says he loves practice is clearly a little "touched." Practice is a time of mutual suffering, of failure after failure in the face of scathing critique. Any women's basketball player will say the same. Strength and conditioning is an awful, painful process. Getting chewed out by a coach in front of fellow players, getting benched, missing the heroic shot at the buzzer—all such growth in learning is difficult and requires the development of ego strength. But out of that shared experience of pushing beyond their limits, all these teams build deep friendships with one another, as well as a belief that they can and will learn from their mistakes—and, at some levels, *only* from their mistakes. They learn what every trained actor knows, that there are no small roles, only small players. And they are all drawn together in the first place by a shared love of the enterprise, whether it be sports, forensics, theatre, music, art, photography, or creative writing.

Obviously, these aspects of character that creative writers also have to develop are immensely important in the business world. Wherever any English major goes in the working world, he or she will have to begin a new learning process at the bottom of the totem pole. That learning will always transpire in a series of initial failures; that process will always require them to accept harsh criticism without taking it personally. Supervisors scold. Bosses lose their tempers. Co-workers snipe at one another. Those who survive an entire program of creative writing have learned, at least in the context of their artistic craft, how to look the critic in the eye, as a colleague and co-worker, and say, "Thank you for the help. I see what you mean now. I'll try to do better next time." This is one important reason why we can say that English majors are prepared to be the life-long learners that every industry needs: they welcome criticism.

My colleague Kevin Stein has taught me much over the years about the teamwork dimension of creative writing, not only in his classroom practice but in his own work as a poet. Stein is the author of five celebrated collections of poetry—*Circus of Want* (1992), *Bruised Paradise* (1996), *Chance Ransom* (2000), *American Ghost Roses* (2005), and *Sufficiency of the Actual* (2008). Since December 2003 Stein has also served as the Poet Laureate of Illinois. He is the latest poet in a tradition that began in 1936, preceded by three other Laureates—Howard Austin, Carl Sandburg, and Gwendolyn Brooks—all of whom, like Stein, were innovators in poetic form and strong voices for a greater human solidarity, to return to Richard Rorty's use of the term.

Stein speaks to my students every year about the *process* that goes into his own work as a creative writer, and one of the key themes that emerges every time from the students' questions is that he relies on the good judgment of a small group of trusted friends, the most important of them being his wife, Deb, but also two other poets in particular—Keith Ratzlaff, a creative writing professor at Central College, and Dean Young, a member of the permanent faculty at the Iowa Writer's Workshop. Stein gave me an early draft of the title poem to his most recent collection, *Sufficiency of the Actual*, to illustrate how a writer's trusted collaborators influence the outcome of a work of literature.

The final version of this poem appeared in the September 2003 issue of *Poetry*, the prestigious journal founded by Harriet Monroe in 1912. In the course of the poem's early development, Stein took the following draft to Iowa City, where his friends Ratzlaff and Young sat with him around a long wooden table and went at the poem, crossing out words and writing comments directly on the draft:

Sufficiency of the Actual (draft)

Had I freed the one-legged cricket twitching in spider-webbed twilight,
       I'd become
Patron Saint of One-Legged Crickets Twitching in Spider-Webbed Twilight.
       I'd be Saint of Cracked Song,
Patron of the Incomplete and Longing. But then, saintly though I might be,
       the spider goes hungry.
Anyway, there's already a multitude, patrons of the broken web, unrisen bread,
       lost keys—
so many, this book says, their duties overlap, say, Patron Saint of Fractions.
       (See Incomplete and Longing.)
That's who The Who prayed to, trashing instruments as "Pop Art Auto Destruction,"
       this, Pete Townsend's phrase,
his name itself a line of demarcation. The young like to break things,
       even themselves.
The young like a summer drum you put your foot through: thump worship.
       Jon Entwistle,
The Who's bassist, stored his parts in a wooden coffin box, until middle-age
       donned knee-high socks.
Then he undid the undoing, cobbling five guitars into one he lovingly dubbed
       "Frankenstein,"
Whose name my friend Frank and I shared with it and, well, with Wollstonecraft's
       romantic sci-fi tragic victim hero.
Together, we made a creature the smarty pants party drunks called "Frank-and-Stein"
       from the keg-drenched kitchen.
Aren't we all cobbled of pieces, glued and screwed and strung together,
       ready to snap?
Aren't we all an instrument some huge hand plucks? Aren't we the tune
       autumn lip-synchs to?
And redemption?—Entwistle's estate auctioned "Frankenstein" for a cool
       $100,000.
My friend did ten years in an orphanage. (See Incomplete and Longing).
       Then his mother
remarried a furnace whose pilot wouldn't stay lit, solving nothing.
       Who said anything about solutions?
You've heard the one about the stutterer who falling from a ladder was cured
       of his affliction.
but made suddenly blind. His mother loved him only a little less than booze.
       Out among the roses

I hear the cricket's cracked song, one leg and those two violin wings.
> a song,
What with the moon rising, crickets must sing, even—perhaps, especially—
> if snared.

Sitting around that long wooden table, with beer and pretzels and the trust that exists between colleagues who respect each other's work, Stein listened to Ratzlaff and Young both tell him they did not like the last stanza. Additionally, in the sixth stanza, they crossed out "Then" in the second line and "solving nothing" at the end of line three. On a positive note, they wrote on the top of the first page that they loved the idea of a "patron saint of our foibles, our weaknesses, our needs."

What Stein observes here about the role all his friends play in the evolution of a poem is that they do not so much write lines or insert words, but that they indicate what *doesn't* work for them as readers; they draw his attention in his early drafts to those areas where change could bring improvement. In this case, he made a radical revision in the ending of the poem, condensing elements of the last six lines and inserting them in an earlier stanza. He then decided to close the final version of the poem with a revision of the metaphor of the man on the ladder, who in exchanging one handicap for another acquires a new medium of praise in the midst of his broken existence:

Sufficiency of the Actual (reprinted with permission of the author)

Had I freed the one-legged cricket twitching in the roses'
> Spider-webbed twilight,
I'd become Patron Saint of One-Legged Crickets Twitching
> in Spider-webbed Twilight.
I'd be Saint of Cracked Song, Patron of the Incomplete
> and Longing.
But then, saintly though I might be, the spider goes hungry.

Anyway, there's already a multitude, patrons of the broken web,
> unrisen bread,
Lost keys—so many, this book says, their duties overlap, say,
> Patron Saint of Fractions.
(See Incomplete and Longing.) That's who The Who prayed to,
> trashing instruments
as "Pop Art Auto Destruction," this, Pete Townsend's phrase,

his name a line and demarcation. The young like to break things,
> even themselves.
The young like a summer drum you put your foot through:
> thump worship.

Jon Entwistle, The Who's bassist, stored all his parts
         in a wooden
coffin box, until middle-age donned its knee-high socks.

Then he undid the undoing, cobbling the five guitars into one
         he dubbed "Frankenstein,"
whose name my friend Frank and I shared with it and, well,
         with Wollstonecraft's
romantic sci-fi tragic victim hero. Together, we made a creature
         the smarty pants party drunks
called "Frank-and-Stein" from the keg-drenched kitchen.

Aren't we all cobbled of pieces, glued and screwed and strung
         Together,
Ready to snap? Are we instruments some huge hand plucks?
         Are we the roses
Or a cricket's cracked song? And redemption?—in the end
         Entwistle's estate auctioned "Frankenstein" for a cool $100,000.

Frank did ten years in the county orphanage. (See Incomplete
         and Longing).
His mother remarried a furnace whose pilot wouldn't stay lit.
         You've heard about
the stutterer who falling from a ladder is cured of his affliction
         but made suddenly
blind. What he no longer sees he sings about instead.

Not only did Stein act on his friends' reaction as readers, he completely re-lineated the poem, breaking the long lines earlier and extending each stanza from six to seven lines. He had considered doing that on his own (the seventh line of the first draft above, for instance, is 22 syllables long, followed by a 2-syllable line, and the stark contrast felt imbalanced). But the final impetus for restructuring the lines came from the editorial needs at *Poetry*, in that they can only print a line of a certain length. In 2007, *Poetry* published only 250 out of 90,000 submissions (an acceptance rate of 0.28%), and so their editors logically fall into the same category of the respected colleague whose opinion on revision matters.

The published version of the poem is much more economical in line, and the difference in the two endings is profound:

Version One

You've heard the one about the stutterer who falling from a ladder was cured
         of his affliction.

but made suddenly blind. His mother loved him only a little less than booze.
    Out among the roses
I hear the cricket's cracked song, one leg and those two violin wings.
    a song,
What with the moon rising, crickets must sing, even—perhaps, especially—
    if snared.

Version Two

    You've heard about
the stutterer who falling from a ladder is cured of his affliction
    but made suddenly
blind. What he no longer sees he sings about instead.

Responding to his friends' critique, as well as to his editor's needs, Stein cut the last six lines of the first version and zeroed in on the unifying theme of "the cricket's cracked song." In the final ending, the one-legged cricket songster, redeemed from the spider's web, becomes the broken man who, redeemed from his speech impediment, sings in his blindness. This metaphorically reiterates John Entwistle's resurrection of the pieces of his broken basses into his patchwork "Frankenstein" instrument, and it also echoes the early friendship between the young poet and his friend Frank, who were pieced together in a unifying and healing friendship after the horrid experience of Frank's ten years of parentlessness. Stein chose to feature at the poem's end what his colleagues liked the most: the idea of a "patron saint of our foibles," the intimation that something is at work in nature and in human life that brings healing and recovery, if not some ultimate redemption. What *did* work for his friends became the final ending; what did *not* work was, in a term common in Kevin Stein's poetry of healing, "elided" away.

    According to Stein, to grow as a writer is to become "a person not easily satisfied," someone who is slow to consider a work finished. He suggests that success in creative writing requires "a blend of humility and arrogance":

> One the one hand, you feel like you can't get anything right and you have to keep at it, and at the same time you think you know better than anybody. That's a tightrope that you have to walk. If you give in to humility, you don't take a risk. But if you fall into arrogance, you fall into unknowing self-parody. You don't question, you don't interrogate yourself.

The same is true in all avenues of labor. This ability to seek out informed criticism and to face what does not work is exactly the same quality of leadership for which Anne Mulcahy, CEO of Xerox, has been so widely praised in the trade magazines of business management. The same is true of General Petreaus, who in February of 2007 took charge of all American military operations in Iraq. Petraeus earned a Ph.D. in International Relations from Princeton University, and in his work in Iraq he has surrounded himself with junior officers who also hold advanced degrees in the liberal arts and who are not afraid to tell him bluntly what they believe is not working.

In the summer of 2006, Barbara Kellerman, a faculty member of Harvard's Kennedy School of Government, wrote in *Forbes.com* that General Petraeus's liberal arts background is a model for the education of 21st-century leaders:

> Those who would lead in the 21st century should *not* necessarily chase one of the professional degrees now considered de rigueur--in law and business, for example. Rather they should get the best possible liberal arts education in the most venerable tradition of American higher education.

Even before General Petreaus took over U.S. command in Iraq, he was understood in the business community to be a different type of leader, the type who would solicit criticism from all sides of an issue and who would contextualize problems culturally, historically, and philosophically.

In creative writing, not only does the classroom work as a committee of the whole to criticize and contextualize their work together, almost always a class will divide into sub-groups that meet outside of class, in someone's apartment or in a bar, and they then launch into one another's work in ways that they would not do in front of the entire group. They break into what Stein describes as "a conspiracy of the like-minded" who work together in a climate of maximum honesty to try to identify what is not working in their art. Such collaboration is creative teamwork in its most genuine, universal, and productive form.

The Socially Constructive Side of Creative Writing

In the spring of 1821, Percy Bysshe Shelley wrote in his essay *A Defence of Poetry* that "Poets are the unacknowledged legislators of the world." Though his cryptic words have generated many interpretations, all of them run to the social, political nature of creative writing, and indeed, when our poets, our dramatists, our novelists, and essayists sit down to write, they are often motivated by a vision of how their society can be made better, more often than not by showing in stark terms how their world is disordered in some way. They write of the poor and the disenfranchised, they write of the injustices and horrors of war, they write of the ongoing struggles for equality and dignity among all the peoples of the world. This is a constant in the literature of the English language—from the *Beowulf* poet's vision of tribal honor and self-sacrifice to Chaucer's scathing critique of corrupt clergy in *The Canterbury Tales*, from Wilfred Owen's warning against the glorification of combat in "Dulce et Decorum Est" to Lorraine Hansberry's complex examination of race and class tensions in *A Raisin in the Sun*.

In our creative writing classrooms, in time, students discover not only the aesthetic power of their craft but also the social and the ethical dimension of their writing. Young people do have something to say about making their world a better place. Nevertheless, no writer I know of is happy to be pigeon-holed as any "type" of writer, least of all a political one. The poet John Keats wrote in a letter to his friend John Hamilton Reynolds (Feb. 3,

1818) that "We hate poetry that has a palpable design upon us," but at the same time, he had something to say about where people should look to find happiness; he had something to say about the universal human experience of losing in death all those we love and the human need to find consolation in the beauty of the material, natural world around us. Literature still serves the dual purposes to please and to teach, even in its least didactic and expressive forms. Even when we can find no clear sense of what the author might have meant, we are still challenged to examine ourselves and the world in which we live.

That element of constructive social criticism, of the examination of the good and the bad in our lives, is always a part of a course in creative writing. Professors of creative writing do not need to design assignments that draw out the political thought of their students, that almost always comes naturally when young people sit down to write. The role of the teacher then is to draw limits to the social critique, to help the student avoid the trap of turning a poem or an essay or a story into what Kevin Stein will sometimes describe as "a bad letter to the editor," something given over more to emotion than to artistic craft.

Creative Writing is for Everyone

In his years as Illinois Poet Laureate, Stein has traveled throughout the schools of the state trying to promote the genre of poetry in the hearts and minds of young people, to inspire them to try their hand at writing poetry themselves and to discover their own voices as writers by exposing them to the voices of the poets of Illinois past and present.

In his efforts to reach young people before they are taught to hate poetry, his website, poetlaureate.illinois.gov, has three links that reach out to young people. One of them, "Youth Poetry," is a link in which he posts poems by schoolchildren from around the state. A fourth grader from Chicago, for instance, has the following poem on the same website with the poetry of such accomplished writers as Lisel Mueller, John Knoepfel, and Susan Hahn:

> I go outside like a wild animal.
> Having snowball fights,
> Wrestling like a real live wrestle,
> Skating on the cold, freezing water,
> Falling, running, jumping, racing.
> I fall:
> The cold wind
> Hitting me in the face.
> I love winter.

This poem shares some of the finest qualities of the imagistic poetry of the early 20th century: the economy of line, the subtle alliteration and the rich cadence of line three as a spondee in the third foot slows the line down at the end, a rhythm that gets repeated in the next line; the creative use of the colon to tie the poem down for a moment in a dramatic pause; the universally human sensory detail of cold as the poem comes to its joyful affirmation at the end. This is a genuinely moving piece of art, reminiscent in its simplicity of William Carlos

Williams's influential 1923 poem "The Red Wheelbarrow" in the way it lets the items of the scene lift the reader, in very few words but with a close attentiveness to the sound and the rhythm of the language, giving both poems the *feel* of a Japanese haiku. The 4th-grader's poem, however, has more "idea" in it than just the "things," which was, as far as we know, not Williams's intent.

Too few people ever get the opportunity to take a creative writing class. Even if one is lucky enough to be at a college that has a program, class size has to be limited to a workshop level, and so willing students are inevitably and regretfully turned away. But in the last forty years, the amount of creative writing being taught in colleges has grown dramatically, and in all likelihood it will continue to grow. A 2005 study of university creative writing programs by the Associated Writing Programs organization showed that in 1975, the United States had only 80 degree-conferring programs. By 2005 there were 720, an increase of nearly 1,000% over thirty years. At the undergraduate level, that growth has resulted in 86 B.A. or B.F.A. programs and 318 schools that offer a minor in creative writing.

Increasingly, college students do have access to the character- and creativity-building practice of the discipline of creative writing. This growth in opportunity has led many who are not English majors themselves to enroll in minor programs, and it is common to find a creative writing class peopled with majors from business, elementary education, engineering, theatre, and the sciences. Everyone stands to gain from the experience of creating their own literary vision of the world, even were they to work in solitude, but with the wealth of input, the wealth of criticism and encouragement that comes to someone in a writing workshop, much more can be accomplished.

The *Harvard Business Review* call for an Executive M.F.A. in creativity makes perfect sense, but until such programs exist, those who are looking for creative thinkers in the ranks of their employees would do well to solicit résumés from graduates in the creative arts, and in particular the art of Creative Writing. When such M.F.A. programs *do* exist, no doubt they will include workshops in poetry, fiction, and drama, because it will always be true that there is no better way to express something that really matters than to tell a story.

CHAPTER 6:
Workplace Internships—
The Application of the Skills Set

The Importance of Internships

Any career-center advisor is always happy to clarify to college students the overwhelming importance of workplace experience to the process of getting a job out of college. If engineers, for example, attend a professionally accredited program, the employer already knows, essentially, what the student's education has been. What employers look for instead is primarily the graduate's internship and work experience, as well as any significant projects that candidate might have done in upper-level course work, usually as the member of a team.

Albeit for very different reasons, the same is true for English majors. Employers do not interview English majors at job fairs about the specifics of their knowledge of American or world literatures; they do not ask for portfolios of literary analyses or collections of expository essays or creative writing. Instead, they come looking for students who are able to show that their English skills are transferable to productive work. This is not to denigrate what we do in the English classroom; it is simply to recognize that our classroom activities are the *means* to a practical end, and not the end itself. In order to demonstrate that those transferable skills are in place, every English graduate seeking a job needs to have had at least one kind of workplace experience, and in recent years, more and more employers are looking for two formal internships before they consider a candidate.

Types of Internships

For an English major, the term "internship" needs to be fairly loosely defined. It operates best as a broad umbrella term that includes both formal internships and informal work roles (various volunteer positions in organizations not overtly defined as "intern"). For example, a student who wants to develop newsletter skills might offer to help with the communications in a social service agency or a local school. A student who is considering a career in web-editing might offer to help any local business advance the effectiveness of their corporate web pages. Students who would consider a career in fund-raising (also called 'development' or 'advancement') might offer their services as grant researchers in any of the grant-driven offices that support people in need in any urban or rural area (after-school programs, public health agencies, shelters of all kinds).

The problem is not that internships are not available; the problem is that English majors do not understand the profoundly deep usefulness of the skills they use every day. Hardly anyone ever speaks of it in the classroom, and so they rarely themselves have the confidence necessary to offer their services to the community.

Allow me, then, to give two examples of successful internship experiences with which I have been directly involved. Both of these former students hope that their successful experiences might help others locate similar opportunities of their own.

Grant Writing

Marilou Niggemann was a student in my Senior Project course in the fall of 2006. Having decided that she wanted to pursue a graduate degree in Public Administration, she asked me if I could help her find a suitable internship for the fall and spring. I then called a former student of mine who had himself been a grant-writing intern as a Bradley English major, Bobby Courtney. Bobby was at that time working as a Strategic Planning Specialist for OSF Healthcare, the same institution that first hired him on as a grant-writing intern. He explained that he could take Marilou on as an intern, but that she would learn more if he could arrange for her to volunteer with the United Way. He knew of their need because he had just been made the chair of the agency's Health and Rehabilitation division. Bobby then set up a meeting with the local Vice-President of the United Way, Don Johnson, to see if he would be willing to hire an intern. As it turns out, Mr. Johnson had been accustomed to working with interns in a series of previous management positions, and he was happy to create a position for Marilou.

Marilou began work before the fall semester was over, learning the nature of the granting process and studying the exact requirements for a grant submission. She was then attached to a local health-care provider that had just been given United Way status as a fundable agency, the Cancer Center for Healthy Living. Marilou then worked with the administration at CCHL over the winter break and into the early spring to help them strategize and craft their first United Way grant application.

Once that stage of the internship was over, Don Johnson brought Marilou in as an observer in the decision-making processes for the healthcare unit of United Way giving in the Peoria area. All in all, the United Way distributed $4.9 million in that annual cycle, including a successful grant submitted by the Cancer Center for Healthy Living. Don Johnson was especially happy with the success Marilou had achieved in the first stage of her work. "The new internship program allowed the Cancer Center for Healthy Living to gain a better understanding of our entire grant process," Johnson points out, "and I'm sure it helped them receive their first grant right out of the box."

Marilou was then brought in on the "Success by Six" early literacy program, the purpose of which was to determine which of three national reading programs would be best for the Peoria community. She then read and analyzed the websites and the books of those three most widely used programs in the country. She also uploaded a request for information on an electronic United Way national posting board. She received responses from United Way offices in Oklahoma, North Carolina, and Minnesota who let her know 1) what program they used, 2) whether they liked the program, and 3) whether they would recommend it to other regional United Ways. Again, in this aspect of her work, Marilou put to work every element of the English skills set.

After completing her work with the Cancer Center for Healthy Living, Marilou created a tool for grant reviewers referred to as a "logic model." This tool was especially important for new volunteer reviewers, to help them understand how to rank grant submissions accurately in the area of education. To begin, she created two fictional agencies, one a day-care program, one an after-school program, and then she created two fictional grant submissions—one very good and one very poor. The most important page of each fiction submission is the "landscape page," a page that explains what the program is, where it is, what it does, and whom it reaches. Underneath that comes a chart that states as many as five targeted goals (e.g. improve math skills, improve test scores, etc.). That, in turn, is followed by a plan for reaching those goals and a system for measuring success. The landscape page is the most important place for an agency to explain their plan for improving on their mission; therefore, the better the picture they paint in words, the better their chance of receiving full funding. Thus it is vital that United Way grant reviewers be able to understand an agency's landscape page.

Marilou's assignment was to imagine fictional education programs, to put herself in the person of two different grant writers: one who knew what she was doing and one who did not. Her fictional submissions were then used in an actual training program for grant reviewers in the Educational division of the Heart of Illinois United Way. The volunteers were given the pages and asked to grade them in a rubric system with a scale of 0-12 as a test to see if they would catch the shortcomings that Marilou had inserted by design. They then compared their actual assessments against a model of proper assessment to see what they still needed to learn about grant-application analysis.

In this part of her work as a United Way intern, Marilou tapped into her experience as a Creative Writing minor. She invented the programs, their names, and their goals. She also created the language that presented the fictional grant-writers as skilled and unskilled in their ability to complete a United Way grant application. This is a perfect example of how, at multiple levels, the skill of empathy allows a trained writer to produce useful and important written reports and tools in the real world of work.

Once the logic-model exercise was completed, what followed next was a joint critical-thinking exercise between Marilou and the "Success by Six" project manager. Marilou first designed and completed a chart that compared the three national reading programs through the lens of a large set of questions, including

- "What is the mission statement?"
- "In what languages are the books available?"
- "Are the books appropriate for urban schools? Rural schools?"
- "What is the cost of the programs, both initial and long-term?"
- "What awards or recognitions the program have received?"

Once the date for the different programs were determined and organized, Marilou created a presentation packet of her analysis that included a cover letter, an individual analysis of each of the three programs (including a list of general information and a list of pros and cons), and a recommendation of which program she would choose, complete with a detailed rationale. She was required to present her packet to the twenty members of the "Success by Six" committee.

In this portion of her internship, Marilou was called upon to read and analyze a sizeable body of text, to work collaboratively with her supervisor, and then to relate to a group of strangers in an oral presentation. In the very structure of the activities, her work was different from the English literature classroom only in the nature of the reading. Because of the very direct way in which Marilou exercised all areas of English Studies in her United Way internship, her final report on her experience has become the binder most often consulted by Bradley students in their own search for internship opportunities. Don Johnson now is an outspoken advocate for English majors going into social-service development. "I believe an English major," he says, "is better prepared to be a successful grant writer than those students coming fresh out of a social-work background."

Marilou's Senior Project course not only led her to her internship, it also led her to discover a graduate program that appealed to her growing desire to work in public service (she had originally planned on a career in Library Science). The first opportunity she discovered was the State of Illinois Legislative Internship Program, but along with that she also discovered the Graduate Public Service Internship Program (GPSI) at the University of Illinois at Springfield. Having studied both options, Marilou chose to apply for the GPSI program because they allowed her to pursue her Master's in Public Administration (M.P.A.), tuition free, while working on stipend with a state government agency. The Legislative Internship Program, on the other hand, did not involve simultaneous graduate education. Furthermore, the M.P.A. program offers a certification in non-profit management. That opportunity was her main reason for choosing the University of Illinois at Springfield over a series of other opportunities.

Her applications for MPA programs stressed heavily her work history with the United Way, and her supervisor's recommendation indicated in great detail that she was experienced in the analytical and communication needs of a future leader in public service. The result was that she was accepted into her first-choice program, and she was offered interviews for 18 other positions within the Illinois state government.

She finally chose to serve with the Illinois Department on Aging. Within that department there is a program called "Grandparents and Other Relatives Raising Children," and in 1999 the state agency published a 30-page book on "starting points" for those people who are either raising children for the first time or for the first time in many years. This book offers resources to the relative caregivers as an initial jumping off point. It also organizes a series of agencies that can support their needs. Marilou's first job was to edit, revise, and update that book. Though the revision is not yet complete, Marilou has added twenty new pages, including a five-page section on coping with incarcerated parents, materials on special-needs children, and an expanded resource directory. She also was able to offer a good deal of editorial change. The completed book will ultimately be issued to thousands of Illinois citizens serving as relative caregivers.

Now well on her way to a career in public service, Marilou Niggemann has a clear sense of the connection between her preparation in college English and her work in Illinois State government:

> For me, English is the basis for everything. I continually refer back to my education and my experiences as an English major. Constantly in my daily work, I look at things more critically. I have found that the simplest word changes can heighten a project as a whole. And the same is true in my daily life. I understand everything I do more deeply, and I am constantly asked to explain the underlying themes behind movies and books and any form of entertainment. I would not be where I am now without being an English major, and I like where I am.

Communications and Global Purchasing:

Another of my students, Melissa Carter, majored in English with an unusually keen sense of where she wanted to go as a student, and thus she took a number of business courses in addition to her English major, and through Bradley's Career Center, she sought out and secured a series of key internship experiences before she had even begun her senior year. In the summer after her junior year, she applied for a paid internship in Communications in a major manufacturing company. In that work, she created an informational and structural format for a new divisional webpage, she generated human resources reports, and she assembled participant binders for the division's Executive Office Review for the CEO and other top management.

Those aspects of Melissa's internship drew mainly on her skills in analysis and writing, but she also had to use her interpersonal skills in group discussion when she was asked to help facilitate a focus group with hourly workers in order to understand their attitudes toward an initiative that was just being implemented in their plant. Her empathetic response to the resistance of the focus group members was essential to success. "I knew that the process that we were trying to implement was necessary from a business perspective," she says in retrospect, "and that it would eventually make their jobs easier. However, it was met with a lot of resistance, as the reasons behind it had not yet been clearly communicated to them because we were so early in the process. The ability to listen to their concerns and be respectful of their attitude towards the changes was necessary in order to help the team create a more effective communication plan."

Throughout her senior year, Melissa worked in the Global Purchasing Division of that same company, this time specializing in the purchasing of aluminum-cast engine parts. We can say with a fair degree of certainty that she was the only English major in America specializing in the international purchasing of aluminum parts for engines. And few English majors anywhere could have found more satisfaction in their work than Melissa did in that unforeseeable internship position.

One reason why Melissa enjoyed this second internship so much was that it called much more heavily on her interpersonal skills in communicating with teams of people, not only in Peoria but around the world. She began by working with teammates from Logistics—as well as with Aluminum Casting partners in the UK and many other sites in the United States—to complete the detailed work of assigning product codes to 5,000 engine parts that the company purchases from its suppliers. She was trained to analyze manufacturing processes by reading engineering prints for engine parts, and she learned how the company builds and maintains its relationships with its vendors by accompanying supply-chain management engineers on two site visits.

What excited her so much about this internship was that she proved to herself she could learn very technical things of great commercial importance, and she discovered that she enjoyed the entire social dimension of this area of international business. No English major comes to college and says, "I really want to specialize in global purchasing." Business majors don't say that either, for that matter. From her first internship in Communications, Melissa discovered that she wanted to work with the actual products the company manufactures, and she was in a position to convince a skeptical program coordinator that they should give her a chance, even without a college major in business or engineering. What we see in Melissa's experience is that by virtue of her excellent interpersonal and communication skills, she not only proved that she could learn in a very serious professional role in a major international company, but that she could thrive.

For her Senior Project course in English, in addition to reporting on her experiences in Global Purchasing, Melissa interviewed with employers at Bradley's Fall Job Fair, and those on-campus interviews then led eventually to competing job offers from 1) a major food products company, where she was offered an excellent position in the marketing division, and 2) a major financial services firms centered in the Midwest. Melissa was especially attracted to the broad training program offered by the financial services firm, in which she would work in all four major divisions of the company in her first year, during which process they would determine where she showed the greatest aptitude and eventually place her in an ongoing position there. Melissa made the decision to commit to that company in November, six months before graduation, and she is very happily working for them to this day.

How to Locate and Apply for Internships

There are many on-line employment sites on which to search for both paid and unpaid internships. Some are free to the user and some require a fee. Most college and university career centers will offer a variety of on-line tools for job searching, and it takes time to learn how to tailor searches for any individual, and for English it can seem especially daunting at first.

As an important component of Affirmative Action law, internships need to be advertised, whether they are paid or unpaid. That said, many companies would be willing to hire an intern (especially an unpaid one) but have never even considered the possibility. Thus, for many years, self-starting English majors have successfully created volunteer positions for themselves by literally knocking on the doors of the kind of businesses that they would like to work for in the future and proposing themselves as potential interns. Over the years I have seen this happen many times—typically at small, locally owned companies like law offices, advertising and marketing firms, and small publishers—and often, once that intern was through, the company continued to be willing to accept interns in the future.

What everyone involved does need to know, however, is that while the creation of a new internship position is a positive thing for everyone involved, it is a position of employment and it needs to be publicly advertised so as not to discriminate against other qualified candidates who might be interested in that position, even if the position is unpaid. Most any college will have a career office or a career counselor who can make it easy for the company to post the internship in a way that complies to Affirmative Action need, and the worst that could happen would be that more applicants might appear, allowing the employer either to expand that labor pool or to make the position competitive in some way.

The Question of Course Credit in English

As I mentioned in Chapter 1, Bradley University has long had in place a practicum course in English for students who are willing not only to use their English skills to contribute to local for-profit or non-profit business, but who also to keep a detailed record of what skills they used each day and how they used them. Traditionally, the term "practicum" was used strictly for courses in which educators or clinicians performed practical tasks in their fields with the supervision of an academic authority of some kind. The word, in fact, derives from the Latin *practicus*, or "practical." Student teaching for education majors is a traditional type of practicum, as are clinical rotations in psychology, nursing, and medicine. At Bradley, we approach the term the same way, but we see any job that requires the English skills set as a job in the field of "English." Thus, students are supervised by their boss in the workplace, as well as by the professor who helps the students with difficult questions and who also helps them to understand and to articulate how the tasks at hand drew upon their skills as English majors.

Other colleges and universities have their own ways of encouraging students to apply their skills in the workplace before graduation, and they offer credit in a number of different ways, whether as general co-op credit or as credit within a discipline. Not all English Departments, however, take part in this important process. The ready availability of internships may be one of the best indicators of an English Department's commitment to their majors' transition into the workplace after graduation. However, many of the finest liberal arts colleges in the country, although they may have outstanding career-center services, offer nothing within the department, no departmental structure that helps their students make the uncertain transition to any future but further study in English.

English majors who are not going to be educators can, of course, find work without being able to articulate how their English major prepared them for their chosen career. They can also find work without having had a chance to demonstrate those skills as a part of their major. Nevertheless, if two students with the same skill level are competing for one attractive position, and only one of those two has demonstrated relevant experience, we know who will be offered the job. Furthermore, if only one of those two candidates is prepared to explain why on earth that employer would ever hire an English major, the employer will in all likelihood hire the student with the more developed sense of self. Here is where we see the importance of an English Department choosing to get actively involved with their majors' futures, rather than standing on the sidelines and passively watching.

An Innovative Approach:
The Business Scholars Program at Hanover College

One of the most creative and exciting approaches to the issue of how college students bridge the gap between a liberal arts major and a career in business is to be found at Hanover College, a scenic liberal arts college in Southern Indiana. I was first introduced to Hanover by Thomas Hellie, the President of Linfield College in Portland, Oregon. In his former role as the President and Executive Director of the J.S. Kemper Foundation, Dr. Hellie supported the development of Hannover's "Center for Business Preparation," or CBP. The Kemper Foundation offers financial grant support to educational programs that share James Kemper's philosophy, available on the Foundation's website, that "a college-level education in the liberal arts represents the ideal preparation for life and work, especially for careers in administration and business," and this is precisely what Robyne Hart, the CBP founder and first Executive Director, was arguing when she began Hanover's process of phasing out the Business major and replacing it with the Business Scholars Program. The program today is supervised by Jerry Johnson, Chairman of the Board of Mercantile Bank Michigan, who as a former member of Hanover's Board of Trustees supported the CBP from its inception.

The Center for Business Preparation initiated its first Business Scholars class in 2004. From the outset, the CBP created a competitive program, and the Business Scholars have had to apply and be selected for participation. The program itself integrates a standard college major in the liberal arts and sciences with two other significant components: 1) a curricular core of seven classroom courses—including a required course in Economics and one in Statistics—one of which is a workplace internship specially designed for each individual student's gifts and interests and 2) a set of mandatory co-curricular requirements designed to prepare them to make the jump into a career immediately upon graduation. The Business Scholars themselves may move into any kind of work—biology research science, for instance—but they all begin their career paths with a solid foundation in "business" issues of all enterprise.

The Business Scholars Curriculum

The Business Scholars program as currently implemented begins in the sophomore year, with "Management Concepts" (CBP 211), a broad-ranging course in the fundamentals of business management, with a special methodological emphasis on case studies through which the students come to understand the theoretical concepts by examining real-world examples. Like many introductory business courses around the country, CPB 211 requires a course in Economics as a pre- or co-requisite. Thus, from the outset in the program, these students are studying business theory and application in addition to their major course of study in the liberal arts.

"Management Concepts" is then followed by a course titled "Financial Decision Making" (CBP 311). This course emphasizes not the mechanics of accountancy but rather the human relations and critical thinking that underpin the financial statements of any business. Once this course is complete and the students have completed a competency exam in computer applications vital to business, each CBP Business Scholar moves on to a research project that will prepare him or her to work in a paid summer internship arranged by Betsy Johnson, the Director of Internships for the CBP. Internship stipends so far have been shared between the program, the host companies, and grant support from the Eli Lilly Foundation.

In this preparatory research course, the students research not only the history and operations of the company where they will intern, they also study that company's industry as a whole, as well as the company's immediate competitors in the marketplace. They also begin to collect data and to think critically about their findings *before* they relocate to the company for their actual summer internship.

The internship itself (CBP 357 "Project-Based Internship") is not a typical work co-op experience, in that the CBP faculty and staff work closely with on-site supervisors to guide the students in their work. More importantly, Business Scholar interns—majors in seventeen different liberal arts majors to date, including Philosophy, English, and Art History—come to the internship heavily prepared by both their curricular and co-curricular training in the program. This internship experience is the heart of the program, each student's opportunity to put business theory into practice by using their liberal-arts training as analytical thinkers with excellent communication and interpersonal skills.

Rightfully proud of their interns' achievements, the CBP has descriptions of all their students' project-based internships available at http://cbp.hanover.edu/scholars/internships. php. Most pertinent to this book is the work of the English majors. In the summer of 2006, for example, Tyler Punt did an internship with the Engineering Contracting firm Shiel Sexton. Tyler did market research to help the company consider opportunities to expand their business into the marketplace in higher education.

In the summer of 2007, English major Deb Celizic worked for the *State of Affairs* show with Louisville's Public Radio station WFPL. A CBP faculty member asked her if she would be interested in an internship in radio because of her interest in music, but as she explored possibilities, she discovered the opportunity at WFPL. Her interview with the show's producer, Robin Fisher, revealed that she would be able to do research and write about issues that mattered to her personally, and she could tell that it would be easy to learn from Ms. Fisher, so the decision was easily made.

State of Affairs itself is a morning call-in show that airs Tuesday through Friday. Deb's primary duties were 1) to research show topics, 2) to summarize this research into "notes" that the host used when speaking with guests and callers, and 3) to utilize this research to construct enticing "blurbs" for the show's website that would encourage people to listen and to call in. As an added bonus as an intern, Deb was trained to use "call software" so that she could screen calls and summarize their questions and their comments for the host to use on the air.

In addition to her work with *State of Affairs*, Deb was also encouraged to develop independent content of her own for a pre-recorded Sunday-only show *Studio 619*. In this part of her internship she demonstrated the ability to work independently that employers prize so highly. She searched through the media reports for "newsworthy" people, and then she would go through a very familiar process for an English major:

1. she would personally contact a potential guest to determine if that person would be willing to be interviewed;
2. she would research any information that might pertain to the interview;
3. she would develop a set of questions that she believed would interest her targeted audience of listeners.

Only when all of the preliminary research was done, and the information was directed toward an identified audience, did Deb proceed to the actual interview itself. In her time with WFPL, Deb interviewed two people on the air: one was a discussion of a clinical psychologist's newest book project, and another was an interview with a local poet.

In addition to Deb Celizic's English internship, other humanities majors completed a series of diverse Business Scholar internships. A History major, for instance, coordinated activities for the Indianapolis Tennis Championships; a Philosophy major was involved in all the daily operations of the wine industry with the Jean Farris Winery; and an Art History major secured a new collection of art that featured athletics throughout history for the BABYPRO company, and she also initiated the process of developing a new line of athletic and exercise books and videos that incorporate that artwork.

All these students' business internships illustrate perfectly the applicability of liberal-arts skills in the real world of work. These majors all worked as researchers and communicators, as creative thinkers and innovators, while at the same time demonstrating that they are trainable, life-long learners who can acquire the skills and knowledge of a particular industry just as they learned the ways of multiple academic disciplines. Accordingly, 100% of the intern-hosting companies involved with the CBP have agreed to host more interns in the future. Part of that success in placing interns with 49 different companies—including some companies that have already hosted more than one intern—is that the CBP does not attempt to fit a round peg into a square hole: each opportunity is tailored to the skills, interests, and personality of the individual intern. That aspect of the CBP's success would be very difficult for other institutions to emulate, especially large institutions, if only for the human resources necessary to coordinate such "fit" between student and internship opportunity.

In order, then, to complete the curricular requirements of the program, CBP Business Scholars need to complete two approved electives—e.g. "Non-Profit Management," "Marketing Communications," "Buyer Behavior," "Internet Studies"—and a senior capstone course,

"Business Strategy." This last course requires each student to create and execute a team-driven comprehensive strategic analysis in partnership with a local business in the area.

The CBP Co-Curricular Requirements

Computer Competency

When majors in the liberal arts begin to seek their first jobs after college, one of the requirements most commonly advertised for jobs that emphasize writing and communication skills is an advanced facility with the computer programs necessary for the professional presentation of text. By far, the most often requested computer skills involve the Microsoft Office Suite of tools, with primary emphasis on Microsoft Word, Excel, and Powerpoint—though some firms request Publisher and/or Access as well. Whatever the industry, liberal arts grads can be expected on the first day of work to be able to present professional-grade presentation to clients or to in-house management. They are also often expected to be able to synthesize research into spreadsheets or to report to their unit teammates and supervisors in text that is amplified by charts, graphs, and images.

Hanover's Center for Business Preparation approaches this career need with a computer-application competence exam, a requirement that must be satisfied before the students are allowed to represent the program in an external internship experience. The text itself is a diagnostic tool that detects those areas that students need to develop, and then the college offers a series of computer-software workshops the students take at no cost in order to acquire the needed skills. Given that these skills are indeed essential for almost all jobs that involve interpersonal communication, and given that English majors routinely work in jobs that draw upon their writing skills, Hanover's model seems a very practical and commonsensical approach that any English department could adopt, assuming that their campus has support staff able to offer such computer-application instruction for students.

Career Preparation

For CBP Business Scholars at Hanover, working with their college's career center is not an option that they choose to take advantage of or not, it is a co-curricular requirement of the program. Throughout their time in the program, students are required to attend résumé workshops; they attend workshops with alumni on interviewing skills, on networking, on business etiquette and dress; and they identify the kinds of on- and off-campus activities that will allow them to apply and develop the skills that employers need.

Most important of all, they are required to work closely with the professionals in their Career Center. Campus Career staff all over the country struggle to find ways to motivate humanities majors, English included, to use their services long before graduation looms, but the traditional culture of English and other liberal arts majors typically does not encourage students to think about where they are going, only about what work lies before them in the classroom. Perhaps there are English departments out there that *require* their students to work with their campus Career Center throughout their degree programs, but in all my research on English program structure, I have never seen this expressed in a single department website. I assume that most faculty would consider such a requirement wrong-headed on at least two counts: 1) that it is paternalistic, that students need to be mature enough to know on their own what they need to do in career preparation, and 2) that it is completely outside the boundaries of the discipline, that English is exclusively about interpretation of text and the expression of critical thought, not about the application of writing or interpretive skills in the world of work. Hanover's CBP program takes the opposite view. In their structure, a student's universal need to prepare diligently over time for the job search is simply a given, regardless that student's maturity level. In addition, no major is understood to exist in a void, free from having to account for the practical relevance of the discipline to the common good. All CBP Business Scholars know that they are preparing for their career from the time they enroll in the program as sophomores. Accordingly, since the inception of the program, within six months of graduation, 98% of Hanover's CBP Business Scholars were successfully employed or were enrolled in graduate programs.

The Center for Business Preparation was able to accomplish its job-placement goals so quickly not only because of their own efforts in networking, workshops, and message polishing, but because they worked closely with Hanover's excellent on-campus Career Center. Margaret Krantz, the Career Center's Director, has shared with me the data on the first job that each English graduate at Hanover had taken over a period of seventeen years (1992-2008). Amazingly, she was able to get information on all but two of 253 English graduates (a reporting percentage of 99.2%), and out of the 251 students reporting, only two have gone as long as seven months after graduation without taking a job. Twenty of them (8%) went on to graduate school in English, including a few who went on to the Ph.D.; eleven students entered law school (4.5%); twenty-four others went on to graduate school in fields other than English (9.5%); and thirty-eight Hannover English grads moved into education (15%), either as teachers and coaches or as students in teacher-certification programs. We can see, then, that 22% of Hanover's 1992-2008 English graduates went directly on to graduate or professional school and that 15% went into teaching. We can also then see that 63% of Hanover English grads moved *directly* into business, including thirty seven in some area of publishing (14.5%). Those businesses are extremely wide ranging: insurance, banking, marketing, management positions of all kinds, sales, non-profit and community-service jobs. In time, many of the students from the graduate-school and law-school groups will also enter into careers in business and government, and therefore Hanover's student body in English is historically even more drawn to business—regardless the presence of the CBP—than most colleges in America.

The long-standing success of Hanover's Career Center in giving students the job-seeking skills they need helped make it possible the Business Scholars program to *require* career preparation. That cooperation between a curriculum and a campus career center *can* and certainly should be repeated all over the country, and nowhere more so than in Humanities programs like English, where the students are least directly prepared by the courses in their major to approach their first job search.

Leadership Series

Another co-curricular requirement Hanover's Business Scholars program is a set of required experiences in which students meet with business leaders in formal workshops, informal group discussions, dinners, and one-on-one discussion sessions. Since the program's inception, visiting speakers have addressed such subjects as the community effect of bank consolidation, the means by which organizations respond to crisis, and the challenges that family businesses face when trying to remain independent. Beyond the public presentations, Business Scholars have the opportunity to interact with the business leaders who come to campus in order to understand better what goes into high-level leadership in a variety of industries.

Again, this component of the CBP vision is something that any English major could pursue, to some extent, at any campus that brings business leaders to campus. So, too, most campuses have leadership programs of one kind or another that they encourage their students to join. My own university, for instance, offers a Center for Student Leadership and Public Service as well as an Institute for Principled Leadership in Public Service. Similar structures are routinely available to English majors wherever their college or university may be, and those who plan on a career in business—in which a demonstrated potential for leadership can be crucial to being hired—are well advised to get involved with their particular school's leadership programs.

Career Portfolio

The final co-curricular component of Hanover's Business Scholars program is a career portfolio. This is a document the students develop that contains not just their résumé but also examples of their work, internship, and classroom experience that has bearing on their future employment opportunities. Again, this aspect of the CBP model is tremendously important to any English major planning on a career in business. Many English programs require a portfolio of work as a graduation requirement, but the portfolio is modeled as a tool of academic assessment rather than as a tool to be used when searching for a job or applying to graduate or professional school. Typically, English majors will assemble examples of their writing in the different years of their program in order to show how their skills in reading, analytical thought, and writing have developed over the four years. The CBP portfolio looks not backwards, but forwards, and its primary purpose serves not the department's needs, but the student's.

One of the leading universities in this area of career preparedness is Florida State University. An electronic information page on FSU's career portfolio program is available at www.career.fsu.edu/portfolio/, and it includes a link to a detailed bibliography in books and articles relevant to the development of successful career portfolios. At Florida State, a staff of trained professionals spent five years developing their Career Portfolio Program (CPP) before it launched in 2002. A detailed history of the program's development is available in a 61-page evaluation report the university makes available at http://www.career.fsu.edu/documents/technical%20reports/ TR35%20finalreport.doc. Since it has been put in place, it has come to be used by thousands of graduate and undergraduate students, and many departments have chosen to make it a required element of their overall curriculum, including Theatre, Nursing, and Dietetics. The Director of FSU's Career Center, Jeff Garis is a contributing editor, along with John Dalton, author of a very useful 2007 book published by Jossey Bass entitled *Emerging ePortfolios: Opportunities for Student Affairs*, which examines the increasingly important role of such portfolios to students, universities, and employers.

Career centers all over the country offer similar services—e.g. electronic resume hosting, "co-curricular resume" development—but career centers typically cannot *require* students or their faculty to take part in their programs. It is entirely up to English majors, their faculty, and their advisors to seek these services out and take advantage of them.

Implications for Other Institutions

The Enhancement of the English Major with Business Minors

Obviously, I agree with Thomas Hellie's assessment that Hanover College's Center for Business Preparation is one of the most innovative things happening in the country relative to narrowing the gap between a liberal arts education and careers in business. The implications for everyone involved in College English are broad, but they can be brought together under a few key umbrella points:

- **Business Courses.** English majors who are not going into teaching should be encouraged to pursue coursework in business in line with their developing career interests. That might be a traditional minor in such areas (traditional and non-traditional) as business management, finance, marketing, public relations, risk management, and human relations. If a business minor is not available at a given college, then students should be encouraged to develop their own "core" of business courses.
- **Business Internships.** Business-bound English majors should also be encouraged and directed toward a series of experiential learning experiences (internships, externships, volunteer experiences, summer jobs) that allow them to put their English skills set to practical use.
- **Career Portfolio.** The co-curricular, experiential learning that English majors do needs to be written out in ways that allow for easy communication with potential employers. Ideally, this will be some kind of career portfolio that can be passed along in both print and electronic format.
- **Career Services.** English majors need to be led to understand that Career Center services are there for *them*, that they need to participate in on-campus training in networking, interviewing, résumé building, and business etiquette. They need to allow the career professionals on their campuses to help them think through their own career ambitions and to guide them in their pursuit of co-curricular experiences.
- **Putting the Pieces Together.** English majors need to do their best to integrate all the various aspects of their education as "business preparation": their English courses; their general-education courses, including foreign language skills and study-abroad experiences; their leadership experience; their workplace and internship experiences; and their volunteer experiences on and off campus.

On this last issue of an integrated approach to business preparation, CBP founder Robyne Hart published an article in the Teagle Foundation's liberal arts blog that sets the issue in context. Her article, "The Tortoise, the Hare, and a Better Approach to Business Education" (July 31, 2007) argues that business programs and liberal arts programs both miss the boat if they do not offer complementary education in both business and the liberal arts:

> Simply adding internships [to a liberal arts major] neither fully addresses students' need to understand and explore careers nor fully enhances their marketability. Trying to make a business major "more like the liberal arts" undermines the fundamental purpose of both.

Her vision is that the liberal arts major itself remain unchanged and so, too, that business education remain business education, but that both components be brought together in an environment of experiential learning in the real world of work.

The literary metaphor in professor Hart's title speaks volumes about the career prospects of English majors:

> Business education in the past can be described by the fable of the tortoise and the hare; the vocationally trained graduate was fast out of the gate, while the liberally educated person learned quickly and the liberal arts foundation enabled the individual to eventually win the race.

By following this model of combining the English major with coursework in business and a heavy dose of workplace internship and networking, English majors can make great strides in shortening the time it would otherwise take to get started on a career and make early progress advancing to higher levels of responsibility and accomplishment.

Section III
Connecting the Classroom to the Workplace

CHAPTER 7:

Getting an Entry-Level Job with an English Degree

How to Find Available Jobs

Career specialists everywhere routinely try to stress the importance of networking in finding a suitable job. I have heard figures as high as 70% in terms of the percentage of job placements that involved networking at some level. Given that important reality, college graduates in English need to be able to locate the jobs that they are free to apply for, regardless any networking possibilities that might be in place.

Again, the very best place to begin will always be the career center at the student's campus, and the most important time to work with those professionals will be when the student has reached that state of readiness when he or she is truly prepared to explore and engage the actual job market, in all its dizzying chaos. At this point, it is vital that a student's expectations be realistic, that students not feel entitled by their college education to step into a middle-management position. Everyone starts in some basement and works his or her way up the stairs. The important first step for an English major is to know where to look for the entry-level jobs available to them.

Job Fairs

Employers begin looking for English majors to hire as early as the fall preceding their traditional spring graduation. Such employers pre-arrange to come to campus and interview students at what it commonly known as a fall job fair. These fairs happen all over the country, and one does not always have to be a student at that institution in order to register and participate. The great beauty of this system is that these employers plan their human-resource hiring well in advance, and students often accept their first job out of college months before that job begins. This brings such fortunate students a tremendous peace of mind as they head into their last semester of college with a clear idea of what they will be doing next.

I am privileged to work at an institution with a world-class career center. Our career center Director, Jane Linnenberger, and her staff bring employers to campus eleven times per year. They also advertise seventeen other regional and national job fairs to which Bradley students have access. Our career center is an active part of an elite association of centers that includes Northwestern, Princeton, and Stanford Universities, and Bradley extends career services at no cost not only to current students, but to all alumni in perpetuity.

As a professor of English, I have learned a great deal over the years from my colleagues in our Smith Career Center, and it is their impassioned work on behalf of our English majors that has drawn my department in the direction outlined in this book. The first thing they taught me is that students must not expect to find employers overtly recruiting "English" majors. Northwestern Mutual, Accenture, Gallo Wines, and Hewitt do not come to campus looking for students to interpret poetry for them. They *do*, however, come looking for students who by interpreting poetry developed a keen intellect and an ability to think critically and communicate clearly. They come looking for people who are demonstrably *trainable*. They come looking for learners. And the typical way they express this is by listing their jobs as open to "ALL MAJORS." English majors who do not realize this simple fact inevitably feel left out when they examine the list of job-fair employers who come in the fall to hire December and May graduates. Nothing could be further from the truth, however. The only time to feel left out is if the only jobs one is interested in are those jobs that advertise specifically for English majors. Employers in publishing and communications often do this, but they comprise a very small percentage of all jobs that hire English majors.

In a recent fall term, for example, 135 employers came to Bradley's campus to meet with students. Forty-three of those employers advertised that they were looking to meet with all majors; only five advertised specifically for English majors: Allstate Insurance, Caterpillar International, The Steak and Shake Company, Starcom Worldwide (a global media communications company), and Wolters Kluwer (an international publishing company with annual revenues over four billion dollars). Any student who examined only the five employers advertising specifically for "English" would have missed opportunities with forty-three other employers, from Liberty Mutual to Lowe's, from Aerotek to Walgreens.

In addition to those employers advertising for English or for "all majors," other recruitment teams come to job fairs willing to listen to any major who expresses a sincere interest in the company. Though they might not have specifically asked to speak to all majors, sometimes a prepared student can explain to the recruiters exactly why the company might consider him or her as a viable job candidate. Of course, this can only happen if the student has a solid résumé, including a series of extra-curricular experiences that speak to that person's employability.

In addition to the fall job fairs, many campuses offer an additional large, general fair in the spring and a series of more specialized job fairs throughout the year. Of special interest to English majors will be job fairs in government work, sales careers, and careers in the social services. Again, the key for every English major is to determine among the interviewing employers which one looks to be a good match, by virtue of each individual student's personality, values, interests, talents, and experience.

Once an English major identifies which employers seem attractive, then the research process needs to begin—long before the recruiters arrive on campus. If a particular job fair offers roughly 60 employers openly interested in speaking with English majors, the motivated student will then study the websites of each one of those companies, a process that will take significant time and one that has to be planned for. When researching companies, a student needs to examine the tab on the corporate website that explains the nature of the different careers that the company offers. This will often be a tab on the toolbar at the top of the page, or it might be situated in a column of links on the right or left of the page. Wherever it appears, it will say something like "careers" or "jobs" or "employment opportunities."

Frequently a company's homepage will also offer sections that speak to the company's history and philosophy. It may also offer biographical information on company leaders. It will always offer in-depth information on the products and/or services that the company brings to the marketplace. No English major should ever walk into an interview situation ignorant of any such information that a potential employer has made available on-line. At the very least, the candidate runs the risk of giving a bad first impression as someone who lacks common sense, if not maturity and the drive to succeed. From a much more positive perspective, a prepared candidate has a good chance of appearing mature, commonsensical, and informed.

The job-fair process itself can and should be an enjoyable experience for an English major. Recruiters staff booths throughout the day in a friendly, almost carnival-like atmosphere, as young people in business-wear (often for the first time on campus) walk from booth to booth gathering information on companies and sharing their résumés and histories with recruiters who are often not very long out of college themselves. A job fair is a place of concentrated opportunity, a time and place when employers gather to look for all majors, English included, but the students have to be able to explain persuasively why they are the type of candidate the recruiters should consider.

Occasionally an unprepared English major will approach a on-campus recruiter who says something like, "You're an *English* major? Why on earth would we ever want to hire an English major?" It may well be that this person truly holds the discipline in contempt as the useless and silly pursuit of useless people, but it is more likely in such cases that the person is not interested in wasting time with candidates who cannot happily explain the relevance of their own major field of study. Students have experiences like this fairly often, actually, especially when they approach employers who did not advertise an interest in "All Majors." Regardless the circumstance behind the aggressive questioning, any English major should smile and welcome the challenge of speaking to their value as a prospective employee. Any employer who does not see the importance of analytical, interpersonal, and communication skills is already out-of-touch with the reality of business, and their bad opinion or ill will is of little consequence. No English major who has successfully cultivated the skills of the discipline should ever feel defensive or insecure when pressed in such a way.

Employment Search Engines

Traditional job fairs are the only circumstance I know where employers come looking for English majors. In all other normal circumstances, it is the English major who does the looking. Without the help of a trained campus career officer, most college students would have no idea where to go or what tools to use to locate available jobs. As an English professor, I only know what I do because I have worked closely for years with Rick Smith, the Director of Career Development at Bradley University's Smith Career Center. He specializes in serving all our students in the Liberal Arts and Sciences, and I have been his student, year after year, course after course, as he has instructed both me and my English majors in successful and unsuccessful strategies in the uncertain world of the job search.

His first piece of advice is that when English majors look for work, they need to begin with a self inventory of some kind. The need to reflect on their own passions, on what they see themselves being happy doing, rather than necessarily what their parents or anyone else wants them to do. Many career counseling services begin with an intake process that might include a Myers-Briggs exam or the Holland Self Directed Search (SDS) exam. The purpose of this kind of testing is to try to match a person's talents, values, and interests with large-scale areas of career possibility. This can be especially valuable for the type of student who sees a hundred distinct opportunities as equally attractive.

The next step is for the students to pull together all the distinctive elements of their educational and work experience, as well as any significant volunteering and leadership experiences. Those raw materials, then, will serve as the building blocks of a series of résumés that an English major can use to match his or her background to a variety of different types of jobs. I will begin a more detailed examination of the English-major résumé in the next section, but my point here is that before looking for jobs electronically, English majors need to know what they are looking for, and that comes from a diligent process of self examination and self discovery. Only then will an English major be in what my colleagues in Career Services refer to as an "individual state of readiness," an expression they share with military trainers and healthcare professionals. Many people who need help can only act upon that help when they are "darned well ready."

Once an English major is truly prepared to look for work, a number of powerful search tools are available for locating jobs, but like any serious research tool, these search engines require training and experience in order to be used to maximum benefit. Many of the most famous search tools, Monster.com for instance, are not the right tool for the traditional 22-year-old college graduate in English; these tools are intended primarily for job candidates with a great deal of experience in particular fields. English graduates who use only Monster run the risk of the kind of employment despair expressed in the Broadway hit song "What Do You Do with a BA in English?" from *Avenue Q* (Music and lyrics by Robert Lopez and Jeff Marx):

> What do you do with a B.A. in English?
> What is my life going to be?
> Four years of college and plenty of knowledge
> Have earned me this useless degree.

I can't pay the bills yet,
'Cause I have no skills yet.
The world is a big scary place.

But somehow I can't shake
The feeling I might make
A diff'rence to the human race!

That Lopez and Marx's hilarious song rings so incredibly true to so many is, in a sense, tragic. It is a comic ode to all those students who never learned what tools to use to look for a career. Furthermore, it captures the angst of a graduate who never learned that indeed the skills of the English major *do* matter. It's the voice of the student whose English faculty wanted nothing to do with his or her life outside the classroom.

All that angst is pointless, however, because not only are the jobs out there, but there are marvelous tools for searching for them. The search engine that my university's career center currently chooses as their primary tool is eRecruiting. This is a service purchased by Bradley University not only for the use of all our current students, as I mentioned earlier, but also for all our alumni. It allows students to search for currently available jobs in a myriad of ways: by job title, by region (including by zip code), or by type of job (full-time/part-time, paid and unpaid internships). It allows students to apply on-line, and it allows them to create a personal profile that searches for jobs automatically.

Any English major, at any time, can search key words like "edit" (which will cover all hits for "edit," "editorial," and "editing") and see what jobs are available in any particular city or region. At the time I am drafting this chapter, "edit" brings up 27 jobs in New York and 5 in Chicago. The search term "write" generates 88 jobs in New York and 36 in Chicago, and this is during the first week of November, not necessarily the key time that employers seek out new employees. Though one might expect these two search terms to generate job openings in the publishing industry, the reality is far from that expectation. The jobs include an opening with EchoStar's (Dish Network's) management training program and an opening for an "Event Planner/Designer/ Marketing/Clerical Guru" with a national manufacturing and packaging company, as well as a slew of positions for "analyst" and "administrative assistant" jobs that offer graduates an immediate future full of on-the-job training and the potential for advancement. In other words, the jobs are there for the application, but one must first know how and where to look.

Analyzing Job Ads Open to English Majors

A few years ago, I had one of my English majors, Laura Hinken, run a search through a series of electronic tools to identify all the jobs she could consider applying for in April in the general vicinity of Chicago, not as an actual job search, but merely as a research project to see what she might expect to do when it is time for her to move on in May. She used *e-recruiting*, *idealist.org*, and *aftercollege.com*. She also looked in the subscriber-only website the *National Employment Bulletin*, available to her through the Bradley Career Center. She began by running searches on the terms "edit" and "write, " and in a matter of days, she generated the following top-10 list:

Desirable Job Titles and Descriptions

1. **Job Title**: Associate Writer.   Learning Point Associates

Description:
- Write and prepare materials (including prose, speeches, and PowerPoint presentations) for the chief executive officer (CEO) to use with existing and potential external clients and partners as well as for internal meetings and presentations
- Research, plan, and write proposals for foundation, corporate, government, and other funding sources
- Help the organization meet financial goals by assisting program staff in the preparation of proposals, related correspondence, reports, and other business development documents
- Improve efficiencies by creating, maintaining, and updating organizational capability statements and examples of related experience
- Assist with research activities to identify funding opportunities
- Assist the CEO in writing speeches and developing PowerPoint presentations for external audiences
- Other duties, as assigned

2. **Job Title**: Program Coordinator. Kaplan, Inc.

Description:
The Kaplan Higher Education (KHE) is responsible for writing and editing program applications for state, accreditation, and programmatic agencies related to post-secondary education. The individual will interact with various departments at the Home Office and leaders at the campuses to gather, organize, and present information according to application standards.

Other responsibilities include:
- Research agency regulations and compile a database of best practices and standards.
- Develop clear, concise and detailed applications that satisfy all agency requisites. Applications necessitate both the ability to write narratives and to organize information in charts and pre-determined formats.
- Responsible for educating campus leaders on the application process requirements. Must coordinate with the campus to extract the necessary information while minimizing their involvement in the process.
- Maintain and manage relationships with a cross section of home office departments and campus leaders.

This position reports to the Operations Manager in the Strategic Planning and Analysis group.

Recent graduates with previous writing experience (internships included) are welcome to apply.

3. Job Title: Grant Writer. Children's Home and Aid

Description:
Responsible for the development of selected foundation and corporate grant applications in four Illinois regions served by Children's Home + Aid (80%). Support the development of major public and foundation proposals (20%). Responsible for, in cooperation with the Manager of Grants and Advancement and the Director of Foundation and Government Funding: writing, editing and proofreading grants narrative, conducting prospect research, managing grant files, drafting cover letters, ensuring timely submission of grant reports to funders, tracking prospect contact and grants calendar through Raisers Edge.

4. Job Title: Administrative Assistant. Chapin Hall Center for Children at the University of Chicago

Description:
Chapin Hall is seeking a Administrative Assistant that manages and executes a number of Communications projects and tasks including producing electronic and hardcopy materials by designing and/or formatting, proofreading, and copyediting; developing and managing the organization's mailing/contact database; managing meeting planning and logistics; regularly updating the organization's website; and providing administrative support to the Public Affairs Director.

5. Job Title: Research Associate. American Medical Association

Description:
You will serve as a member of the AMA's Health Information Technology (HIT) Initiatives Team with key responsibility for researching various HIT related issues, authoring reports to AMA staff, and developing informational materials for physicians. Materials include articles, website material and press communications. Responsibilities will include providing direct support to the Director, Health Information Technology, helping research and write reports, working on new programs and activities, preparing communications and responding to both external and internal inquiries regarding HIT related issues. You'll also develop and maintain HIT content on the AMA website, develop member communications to inform and educate physicians on AMA initiatives and policy discussions related to HIT, coordinate with Media Relations and Membership Communications staff to support member messaging strategies

and media communications, and work with AMA staff (e.g., Advocacy, Professional Standards) to develop consistent) to develop consistent key messaging for the AMA on HIT issues.

6. Job Title: Project Assistant. American Society for Clinical Pathology

Description:
The Project Assistant will support the Grants Administrator in financial tracking activities related to the ASCP's cooperative agreements with the Centers for Disease Control to create and provide laboratory training in the PEPFAR (President's Emergency Plan for AIDS Relief) countries. He/she will also provide additional administrative support to the Director, and assist the Director and Grants Administrator in the preparation and submission of grant proposals.

Roles and Responsibilities:

1. Track and monitor project expenses, review travel expense reports, maintain monthly financial tracker, reconcile financial statements, review and coding of credit card statements.
2. Assist in the preparation of project deliverables, i.e., quarterly financial reports and maintain project invoices.
3. Assist in preparing grant application materials for new funding opportunities.
4. Provides administrative support in the planning of conference calls and meetings; travel logistics; and compiling meeting summaries.

7. Job Title: Medical Writer. SG-2

Description:
The Medical Writer will be responsible for the development and writing of educational monographs, and focus reports pertaining to health care and technology innovation.
  • Outline/Development of educational content, including slides and monographs
  • Editing/proofing Sg2 materials for Web and print publications
  • Repurposing previous Sg2 content, such as Briefings and Executive Briefings, into smaller documents, as needed after conferring with content experts on outline development

8. Job Title: Copy Writer. Carle Foundation

Description:
Researches, writes and produces bold, strategic, persuasive and creative messages in all media and in a variety of styles including ad copy, newsletter writing, internet/web page writing, employee and corporate communications and journalistic writing. Meets the communication requirements of clients.

9. Job Title: Copywriter/ Marketing Communications Specialist. Cole-Palmer

Description:
Using established templates and guidelines, the Marketing Communications Specialist writes clear, persuasive sales-oriented copy for—but not limited to—catalogs, direct mail pieces, brochures, space advertising, postcard decks, tradeshow signage, and other sales materials. The MCS is also responsible for writing/editing occasional articles and overseeing production of product press releases, eMedia content and newsletters.

10. Job Title: Associate Editor. Specialty Publishing Company

Description:
Specialty Publishing Company, publishers of 3 national publications is currently seeking a talented Associate Editor with 2+ years experience (preferred, but not mandatory) to join its award winning editorial staff. Responsibilities will include researching, writing, editing, and proofreading magazine departments and features for both print and electronic media.

This list of available jobs was tailored to Laura's love of writing. Although she saw many other jobs for which an English major might apply, these were the jobs that emphasized writing, and upon analysis of the company, they seemed like places that she would enjoy working. We then organized all the stated job requirements into the following series of umbrella topics:

<u>Requirements Listed in Laura's Top-Ten Job Ads</u>

1. **Working Under Deadlines (4 out of 10 ads)**
   • "Ability to work quickly under tight deadlines" (Learning Point Associates - LPA)
   • "Works well under pressure and with tight deadlines" (Kaplan)
   • " effectively set priorities and time allocation" (AMA)
   • "the ability to manage multiple projects within a fast-paced, deadline-oriented environment (Specialty)

2. **Writing Ability (6 out of 10 ads)**
   • "Demonstrated ability to write clear, concise, structured, and persuasive text for a variety of audiences" (LPA)
   • "two years experience in project support utilizing budgeting skills" (ASPC)
   • "excellent written and oral communication skills" (ASPC)
   • "Desired skills in business writing" (SG2)
   • "Researches, writes and produces bold, strategic, persuasive and creative messages in all media and in a variety of styles including ad copy, newsletter writing, internet/web page writing, employee and corporate communications and journalistic writing" (Carle Foundation)

- "Meets the communication requirements of clients" (Carle Foundation)
- "Must be able to translate creative ideas into easily understood communication that generates results" (C. Parmer)
- "Must possess excellent writing, editing and verbal communication skills to write and correct copy and express ideas to others" (C. Parner)
- "excellent writing, editing, and research skills" (Specialty)

3. **Writing Experience (6 out of 10 ads)**
    - "Minimum of three to five years of writing experience, including grants, proposals, educational materials, marketing products, and applications" (LPA, Kaplan)
    - "minimum of three years document production experience including proofreading and copyediting required" (Chapin Hall)
    - "Demonstrated writing capabilities with strong interest in medical writing" (SG2)
    - "Demonstrated proficiency in business writing and copyediting" (SG2)
    - 2-3 years direct marketing experience, with an emphasis on copywriting or a combination of education, experience and /or licensure/certification" (C. Parmer)

4. **Computer Skills (7 out of 10 job ads)**
    - "Proficiency with Microsoft Office suite of products" (LPA)
    - "Familiarity and comfort in use of Microsoft Word, Excel, PowerPoint, Access, and other electronic data tracking systems" (C. Home)
    - "proficiency with software applications and an aptitude for learning software applications related to webpage design, publishing, and presentations required; proficiency in Microsoft Office Suite and working knowledge of HTML, Quark Xpress and/or Pagemaker desktop publishing, and document conversion using Adobe Acrobat software preferred; working knowledge of one or more of the following applications preferred: Dreamweaver MX, Photoshop, Javascript, a text editor program such BBEdit or FTP" (Chapin Hall)
    - "PC literacy expected. Familiarity with software packages, particularly Microsoft Work, Excel, Access, PowerPoint is required" (AMA)
    - "This role also requires intermediate to expert-level knowledge of Microsoft Office programs (i.e., Word, Excel, and PowerPoint" (ASPC)
    - "Proficiency in Microsoft Word and PowerPoint" (SG2)
    - "Must be proficient in Microsoft Office, PC environments" (C. Parner)

5. **Research Skills (1 out of 10 job ads)**
    - "Strong research skills . . ." (AMA)

6. **Analytical Skills (1 out of 10 job ads)**
    - "Strong analytical skills . . ." (Kaplan)

7. **Organizational Skills (6 out of 10 job ads)**
    - "Strong organizational skills with the ability to handle multiple tasks" (LPA)

- "Possesses exceptional organizational skills with the ability to prioritize and multi-task" (Kaplan)
- "excellent organizational skills and attention to detail" (ASPC)
- "Demonstrated organizational skills pertaining to publications project management" (SG2)
- "Exceptional organizational skills to contribute to expanding titles" (Specialty)
- "Must possess excellent organizational skills to be able to handle multiple projects under tight deadlines" (C. Parner)

8. **Interpersonal Skills (5 out of 10 ads)**
   - "Strong client service orientation" (LPA)
   - "capacity to work well under pressure & meet deadlines, ability to communicate effectively w/ diverse groups, cooperate w/ colleagues & manage group project . . . excellent communication and people skills for ongoing interactions" (Kaplan)
   - "capacity to work well under pressure & meet deadlines, ability to communicate effectively w/ diverse groups, cooperate w/ colleagues" (C. Home)
   - "Excellent interpersonal skills are required" (AMA)
   - "Must possess strong interpersonal and presentation skills to work well within a team environment as part of the creative process and must have the ability to build strong relationships with press contacts to ensure press release will be picked up (C. Parner)

9. **Teamwork Skills (3 out of 10 ads)**
   - "Team player who is self-directed and results-oriented" (Kaplan)
   - "manage group projects" (C. Home)
   - "a team player capable of both independent & directed task completion" (C. Home)
   - "Must be detail oriented & able to serve as a helpful, problem-solving representative of the development team" (C. Home)
   - "Must exhibit strong creative ability that is conducive to working with diverse multi-disciplinary colleagues in a wide array of child welfare disciplines" (C. Home)
   - "Must be able to work effectively as a member of a team" (ASPC)

10. **Initiative and Independence (3 out of 10 ads)**
    - "Demonstrated ability to work independently with minimal supervision" (AMA)
    - "Must be able to work effectively independently" (ASPC)
    - Candidate should be a creative self-starter" (Specialty)

In addition to all of these "requirements" solicited by the ten employers, there was also the following finite list of "preferred" elements that they would consider in screening resumes:

- "experience in private post-secondary education is preferred" (Kaplan)
- "education or non-profit background a plus" (LPA)
- "Nonprofit background preferred. Knowledge of philanthropy & program evaluation preferred" (C. Home)
- "writing experience preferred; event planning experience and experience in a public affairs or communication environment preferred" (Chapin Hall)
- "Previous work experience in the fields of health administration, information systems or communications, preferably within a health organization preferred" (AMA)
- "Enjoy working with health policy matters" (AMA)
- "Interest in web page maintenance and knowledge of content management software desirable" (AMA)
- "If you would be comfortable working in a fast paced environment with ambiguity and rapid shifts in priorities, and enjoy a collegial atmosphere--this may be an excellent opportunity for you" (ASPC)
- "An uncompromising commitment to quality and a passion for health care" (SG2)

What we see here from both the preferred elements and from the ten categories of required elements is that these employers are truly interested in hiring someone who has the commonly known skills of a typical English major (writing, communication, interpersonal/teamwork skills) but also the less-discussed skills of being able to work under deadline and the ability to be self-motivating and independent. To me, however, the most striking result of this research is that 7 out of 10 employers listed very specific computer skills as a *requirement* for consideration as a job candidate. What this should tell everyone involved in college English is that our students should seek every opportunity to learn to use as many software products as they can, but especially all the tools in Microsoft Office (e.g. Word, Excel, PowerPoint, and Publisher) and the tools necessary for web communications (e.g. Adobe Creative Suite). These computer skills are not something for an English major to begin to work on in senior year; they are skills they need to master and to use in some constructive way outside of class as soon as they are able, ideally from the freshman year on. This is not simply about presenting a competitive edge in the job search; computer skills matter because the kind of jobs that English majors gravitate toward necessarily use these tools routinely in the daily practice of professional communications.

Designing an English-Major Résumé

Once a set of desirable job opportunities is in place, a graduating English major will then be ready to begin the process of writing a series of résumés that target the finite list of requirements specific to each job ad. This principle is absolutely essential for English majors: a "targeted" résumé, one designed around the particulars of a specific job ad, will be much more effective than a general résumé that the candidate *hopes* will address the company's actual needs.

As a result of Affirmative Action laws, companies are only allowed to screen résumés by virtue of the specific content of the publicly posted job ad. If a skill or a type of experience is listed as "required," then it is not an option for the applicants; they *must* indicate that they have the desired skill or experience in the résumé, or they cannot be considered for an interview. Understanding this reality is essential to understanding the audience and situation of the job application process. Although some employers do violate this law, the law nevertheless exists. For every criterion listed in the ad, the screeners need to assign some evaluation—typically a point total.

The following is a fictional version of a typical résumé screening document:

REQUIRED ELEMENTS (a zero in any category disqualifies candidate)

Bachelor's degree in English or related field _____ pts.
    (No degree in hand = 0)
    (B.A./B.S. English = 5 pts)
    (B.A./B.S. related field = 3 pts)

Writing-intensive work experience _____ pts.
    (No experience = 0)(1-2 years = 5 pts)
    (3 years or more = 10 pts.)

Proven ability to work as part of a team _____ pts.
    (No evidence = 0)
    (Some evidence = 4 pts.)
    (Extensive evidence = 8 pts)

Grant-writing experience _____ pts.
    (No experience = 0)
    (Some experience = 4 pts.)
    (Extensive experience = 8 pts.)

Skilled with Microsoft Office Suite of Products _____ pts.
    (No indication = 0)
    (Some skills evident = 5 pts.)
    (Extensive experience and skill evident = 10 pts.)

DESIRED ELEMENTS (a 0 does not disqualify)

Experience in non-profit business _____ pts.
    (No indication = 0)
    (Minimal experience = 1)
    (Significant experience = 2)

Interest in website maintenance   _____ pts.
    (No indication of interest = 0)
    (Interest indicated = 2)

The résumé-screening committee will pour through all the applications and screen for the points as outlined above. If a hiring criterion is listed as "required," the applicant simply cannot ignore it. Not only has the company indicated that this aspect is *essential* to their job-search analysis, it may also be heavily weighted in terms of points. Consequently, when designing a résumé, an English major should allow more space for those elements that the company has stressed as important.

    As an exercise in the "English" skill of empathy, put yourself in the shoes of a résumé screener. What type of résumé would you prefer to evaluate, 1) one that easily corresponds to the given criteria of the ad or 2) one that is organized in a predetermined set of categories that has little to do with the screening criteria? The question is rhetorical, of course, yet nonetheless a tremendous number of English graduates do not go to the trouble of tailoring their résumés to the job ads for which they apply.

    Given, then, that a targeted résumé will be more effective than a general one, the question still remains of which traditional résumé structure will best suit the job notice at hand. Three options of structural emphasis stand out: education, experience, and skills. A chronological option also exists, but structuring the content of an English major's résumé simply around the order in which education, experience, and skills were acquired will rarely serve the needs of a targeted situation.

Education Emphasis

    For students who have just graduated and who have had very little experience outside of college, a résumé that stresses education makes sense. For example, a student who took classes throughout each summer, without working, and graduated in three years rather than four might look for a job ad that focuses on English educational experience and skills. The Educational Testing Service, for instance, might be looking for people to work on the verbal portions of the ACT and SAT exams. The Sylvan Learning Center might also be looking for someone to step into an individualized educational setting for students with special needs in writing. Or any of the overseas programs looking to train English majors to teach in Japan, Korea, or the Czech Republic might advertise merely for someone with an English degree and an adventurous spirit.

    Regardless the nature of the exact situation, a résumé with an education emphasis will look something like this:

Almetta Chang

Current Address
1313 Mockingbird Lane
Erehwon, MA 11111
(222) 444-44444

Permanent Address
1313 Larry Avenue
Chicago, IL 22222
(333) 888-8888

OBJECTIVE: Seeking a position teaching English in the Czech Republic.

EDUCATION:
B.A. in English. Smoot University, Smoot, Wyoming.   *(May 2010)*
>   (Minors in Russian Language and in Eastern European Studies)

A.A. in Liberal Arts. Blue Mountain College, Brunswick, ME.   *(May 2008)*

RELEVANT COURSES:

Senior Project (English 499) on Teaching English Overseas   *(Spring 2010)*
- Interviewed and networked with English instructors overseas.
- Assembled report on all overseas teaching opportunities for English graduates.

LAS 301 Internship / Co-op   Kids Learning English Program   *(Fall 2009)*
Job Title: Student Advocate
- Gave individualized language instruction to students aged 12-18 as intern for the K.L.E.P. program.
- Served as part of grant-writing team to pursue additional resources for the program.

Senior Project (Eastern European Studies 495)   *(Fall 2009)*
- Researched and gathered print and electronic sources pertaining to Czech culture, economics, politics, and education.
- Synthesized research information into PowerPoint presentation delivered to Smoot's Economic Development Council as part of a series on trade issues.

RELEVANT EXPERIENCE:

Smoot University Tutor (September 2007 - May 2009)
- Provided tutoring in Russian, calculus, and composition to international students.
- Chaired committee that implemented new curriculum design in language tutoring.

SKILLS

- Fluent in Russian; reading competency in Spanish.
- Highly experienced with Microsoft Word, Excel, PowerPoint, and Publisher.
- Working knowledge of Web-design software (Adobe Creative Suite 4).
- Trained and experienced in business and technical writing.

This résumé targets an ad that asks only that the applicant have a degree in English and a willingness to live overseas, with tutorial experience as a "plus." Therefore, the fictional Ms. Chang only shares the experience she acquired at her two colleges, and in particular only those elements of her education and experience that speak to her potential as a tutor. Beyond her tutoring experience, she also features her ability to work as a member of a team (and as a team leader) in grant-writing and curriculum development, and she gives evidence of her ability to present her work publicly and professionally. Even in 12-point Times New Roman font, this résumé fits easily into one page.

Experience Emphasis

Most jobs that English majors apply for, however, will not stress education in their key criteria for hiring. Instead, they will identify required experience and/or required skills, often implicitly by simply listing the tasks and responsibilities of the position. The following fictional job ad—a posting that makes no mention whatsoever of college major—is probably best addressed by a résumé that features "experience":

Administrative Assistant. The Doughboy Center for the Arts, Sister Bay, CA.

> The Doughboy Center for the Arts is seeking an Administrative Assistant to 1) manage internal and external communications, 2) maintain and improve the Center's website, 3) provide support for the Director of the Center.

Required:

- 1-2 years experience in professional communications, including newsletter writing and website maintenance.
- Experience in all areas of document production: formatting, proofreading, copy-editing.
- A proven track record of performance under deadline.
- Experience working as a member of a communications team.
- A 4-year college degree in any major.

Also a Plus:

- Knowledge of the history and the art of World War One, in particular the role of the American infantryman, or "doughboy."

Although this ad does identify a specific skills set (editing, teamwork, website construction and maintenance), it presents the requirements as a matter of experience and "track record." Any résumé format *could* work to communicate the necessary information for the screening audience, but the situation of the ad indicates that an "Experience" structure might be the most efficient.

When targeting this ad, an English major might well try to imagine what a screening document might look like and structure the résumé accordingly:

Requirements (any score of 0 disqualifies candidate):

Communications work experience w/ newsletter and website work:
        (No experience offered = 0 pts)
        (Less than 6 months = 2 pts)
        (7-12 months = 4 pts)
        (13-18 months = 6 pts)
        (19-24 months = 8 pts)

Experience in document production:
        (None indicated = 0 pts.)
        (Some experience = 4 pts)
        (Heavy experience = 8 pts)

History working under deadline:
        (None indicated = 0 pts)
        (Some experience = 4 pts)
        (Heavy experience = 8 pts)

Teamwork:
        (No indication = 0)
        (Some experience = 4 pts)
        (Heavy experience = 8 pts)

College degree:
        (No = 0 pts)
        (Yes = 2 pt)

Additional quality (no penalty for 0 score):

Knowledge of WWI history and art
        (No indication = 0)
        (Some knowledge = 1 pt)
        (Deep knowledge = 2 pts)

Any audience/situation analysis like this is always at best merely educated guesswork, but given that the company is required by law to stick to the criteria published in the ad, chances are good that an analysis like this will be fairly accurate.

Assuming, then, that the criteria will be reviewed by screeners in the same order in which they were presented in the ad, the English-major applicant might well choose to structure the new résumé around relevant experience rather than college education:

Joshua L. Chamberlain

ColLawrence65@yahoo.com

OBJECTIVE: To obtain a full-time position as an Administrative Assistant with the Doughboy Center for the Arts.

RELATED WORK EXPERIENCE:

American Legion Post 951, Wantaugh, New York
Communications Intern. January – November 2007
- Developed and implemented newsletter for public schools to advertise Legion scholarships, contests, and events.
- Arranged and facilitated speaking engagements for Legion Commander.
- Chaired a team of Legion volunteers to overhaul Post website. Completed project two weeks ahead of target date.

HistoricLongIsland.com, Manhassett, New York
Associate Editor. January 2009- May 2010
- Worked on a team to copyedit encyclopedia-style articles before posting them on a website.
- Used Dreamweaver, Adobe Photoshop, and Contribute to upload Web content and design elements.
- Wrote and compiled research for pieces on local historical people, places, and events.

New York University, Office of the Dean of Liberal Arts and Sciences
Student Assistant. September 2006 – May 2010
- Performed administrative tasks, including copying, filing, and completing paperwork in a professional setting.

EDUCATION:

New York University, New York, New York
Pursuing Bachelor of Arts in English, to be completed May 2010
- Minors in History and Web Design
- Overall GPA: 3.71, Major GPA: 4.00 on a 4.0 scale
Honors: Dean's Scholarship, Dean's List (six consecutive semesters)

OTHER INTERESTS:
- Son of WWII veteran and silver star recipient, past Commander of American Legion Post 951.
- Life-long enthusiast of military history, including the history of WWI.
- National Finalist in American Legion Essay contest, 2004.

This résumé, very different in structure from the last one, still features the same kind of information about English skills and experiences, but it orders the delivery of the information in the context of the job criteria listed in the ad.

Skills Emphasis

A final strategy for English majors to consider when constructing their résumés is to contextualize their education and experience into a set of skills. This kind of structure makes the most sense when skills are featured prominently in the hiring criteria of an ad. Such ads might read like the following:

Wanted: Legislative Monitor

Manatee Insurance is looking for a recent college graduate to monitor the state legislative activity in Sacramento that affects the local (and national) insurance industry. Our LM builds relationships with key legislative staff, studies legislative activity, and then reports back to our Board of Directors each month to keep the company apprised of changes in public policy and regulation.

Requirements:

- College degree in any area of Liberal Arts or Communications.
- Outstanding interpersonal skills.
- Excellent oral and written communication skills.
- Professional-grade skills with presentation software such as PowerPoint.
- Self-motivated, able to work without direct supervision.
- Able to understand and analyze financial reports.

With this job ad, the easiest way for the screeners to navigate the résumé will be for the applicant at some point to organize the material around a few key areas of skill. Again assuming that the order of the topics in the ad will match the screening device, the applicant might structure the résumé this way:

Emily Allstate

Current Address
1313 Mockingbird Lane
Rio Rita, CA 11111
(222) 222-2222

Permanent Address
1313 Larry Avenue
Rio Rita, CA 11111
(222) 222-2222

OBJECTIVE: To obtain a full-time position as a Legislative Monitor.

EDUCATION:

B.A. English, California State University at Rio Rita. May 2008
(Minors in Political Science and Business Administration)

EXPERIENCE:

The Campaign for a Healthy California (Rio Rita, California)
Organizer (Fall 2009-Early Spring 2010)
- Organized and directed a Town Hall Meeting on health care attended by a diverse audience of 150 people from the Southern California community, including government officials, reporters, and other interested parties.
- Lobbied policy makers, non-governmental organizations, community organizations, small businesses, labor alliances, and others.
- Addressed issues such as insurance premiums and coverage, cost containment, and liability and risk pooling.

Grassroots Campaigns, Democratic National Committee (Sacramento, CA)
Field Manager (Summer 2010)
- Worked on the Presidential election in a key state, raising funds and mobilizing voters.
- Trained new staff in canvassing and skills and helped devise improved strategies.
- Managed canvassing teams in the field, acquiring and apportioning assignments to maximize the effectiveness and success of the campaign.

United States Republican Congresswoman Mary Bono (Palm Springs, CA)
Senior Intern (Fall 2008) *Junior Intern* (Spring 2008)
- Co-chaired a congressional All-Academy Night (Spring 2008)—an informational meeting for high school students in the district interested in attending one of the five United States military academies.
- Conducted casework in various fields, including Social Security, Veterans Affairs, and Immigration.
- Fielded constituents' questions concerning area problems.

California State Democratic Senator Alex Padilla (Sacramento, CA)
Senate Office Page (Summer 2008)
- Staffed the Senate's Education Committee.
- Aided constituents with problems and questions dealing with state-level government.

SKILLS:

Interpersonal
- Excellent listening skills honed in political work and in the literature classroom.
- Able to relate well to people on both sides of the political aisle.
- Work well as member of a team.

Communication

Oral:

- Comfortable and experienced speaking in front of large groups.
- Able to deliver complex materials in clear oral reports.
- Speaking-level fluency in Spanish.

Written:

- Trained and experienced in business and technical writing.
- Able to adapt a message to specific audiences and situations.
- Excellent editing skills.

Computer

- Trained and experienced in PowerPoint, Microsoft Word, and Excel.
- Experienced with the web-management software product Adobe Creative Suite 3.

Business

- Trained in financial analysis in my Business minor, including courses in Statistics, Quantitative Methods, and Finance.
- Understand complex financial reports, especially as they affect public policy.

This résumé does not leave it entirely up to the reader to abstract the desired skills from the list of experiences; it also lays the skills out in the same order they appear in the ad. More importantly, the "Skills" section includes new, important information that would not have come out in the list of co-curricular experiences (computer skills, math capability, foreign-language skills useful in California political work, etc.).

There is no such thing as *the* one way to do something as complex as a résumé. There is no one set of rules that everyone is to follow, only a set of conventions that students need to embrace when adapting their résumés to the needs of a specific job notice. Every campus career center will offer résumé-writing workshops to help students conform to the norms of given areas of work. Some career centers will also help students develop a general, electronic résumé that they make available on-line to employers. I once had a student who received a cell-phone call in class (having forgotten to turn her phone off), and after class she informed me that it was an employer she had never heard of offering her a job in response to the electronic résumé that the Bradley Career Center posted on her behalf. She had already accepted a job in non-profit fundraising, but she was nevertheless flattered. She also then knew to ask the career center to remove her résumé from the list of active job candidates.

No college student should take on the complicated task of applying for a job without the assistance of their school's career center, but especially not English majors, whose path to a specific career is always circuitous. The trick, however, is to understand that the role of the career center is not to apply for a job *for* the students; their job is to teach students how to prepare to apply for the job themselves. Thus, career centers will routinely post announcements of workshops they offer in such areas as "Interviewing Skills," "Résumé Building,"

"Cover Letters," "Networking," "Professional Dress and Etiquette," and "Job-Search Strate-gies." But the Career Services staff can only help those students who seek them out, who already understand that looking for a job requires a unique set of skills all its own.

Career counselors derive as much satisfaction in helping an English major get started on a career as any professors take in their own teaching, but the English major has to be ready and willing to learn. This is where the culture of an English Department faculty can have a positive or a negative effect on student success. If the English faculty at a college cannot articulate the "usefulness" of what they teach, then in all likelihood, the students will not know either. And if the faculty and student body in English cannot tell employers the practical value of what they do, how can they expect their career center to do that *for* them? If a cultural divide exists on a campus between the English Department and the career center, students will have a much harder time getting on with their lives after graduation than they would were they schooled at a campus where everyone clearly understood the utilitarian, practical value of the English skills set.

Transitioning to Workplace Culture

In the fall of 2007, the Illinois State University Marketing Department did something fairly outrageous by college-campus standards: they passed a dress code for their majors, insisting that they had to show up for class in "business casual." Granting that such a policy is problematic at many levels—especially given the fact that "business casual" in some en-vironments means a blue dress shirt instead of a white one—their purpose was to deal with a very real problem, one every bit as common in English as in Marketing. College students everywhere grow accustomed to schlepping to class in unwashed blue jeans, t-shirts, paja-mas, and sweats, with flip-flops on their feet and baseball hats covering their unkempt hair. They arrive late to class or not at all. They hand in work late. Moreover, all of this is ac-cepted as common practice in many areas of university life and has been for decades.

The problem occurs when college graduates are too slow to let go of the laid-back approach to work that they experienced in college. The problem sometimes surfaces before graduation, when students show up to the first day of an internship and are sent home to get "properly" dressed (sometimes in clothes they do not yet own), or when a student arrives an hour late to a summer job without calling in ahead of time and finds herself fired. Illinois State's Marketing Department took unusual measures to deal with the issue of their graduates being unprepared to make the transition to the cultural demands of work after college, but the problem itself is anything but unusual.

Again, enterprising English majors will understand that the culture of the workplace and the culture of a college campus are very different things, and these people will take advantage of the help that their Career Centers offer on such mysterious matters as what the difference is between "business-formal" and "business-casual dress" or where you wear your nametag at a networking event (on the right side, by the way) or how you write an appropri-ate follow-up letter to an interviewer. The necessary training is available at virtually any campus, but English majors first need to come to understand how much good they stand to derive out of working with the professionals in their campus career center.

CHAPTER 8:
Career Paths of English Majors

An English Major's Entry-Level Career Options

As I said in the first chapter of this book, the reason English majors have such a hard time telling people what they plan to do after college is that it could be literally anything. The vast majority of jobs available to English majors, as to any other liberal-arts students, require further specialized training of one kind or another. A few English graduates, in fact, choose to go back to undergraduate school for a degree in Engineering or Accountancy, having discovered at a later age that this is the area of work they desire the most.

One place to begin to see what jobs English majors actually take when they graduate is the "Job Function" list, by curriculum, published in the quarterly salary survey of the National Association of Colleges and Employers (NACE). Each fall, NACE publishes the categories of work that English majors go into directly after college. These data are supplied each year by participating college career centers, the people who do the difficult task of tracking graduates' job placement and salary information. The fall issue each year summarizes the hiring patterns of the previous academic year.

Since 2005, the NACE data show English majors going on to work in all of the following areas:

Accommodation/Food Service Administration (Healthcare)
Administration (Social Services)
Advertising
Agricultural/Natural Resources
Agriculture, Forestry, Fishing, Hunting
Architectural Services
Arts, Entertainment, Recreation

Banking (Commercial)
Banking (Investment)

Building, Developing, General Contracting
Buyer/Merchandising

Communications (Broadcasting/Telecommunications)
Computer & Electronic Products Manufacturing
Computer Systems Design/ Consulting/ Programming
Consulting Services
Counseling
Customer Service

Design/Graphic Arts

Educational Services
Environmental/Sanitation Engineering
Executive, Legislative & General

Financial Services
Food, Beverage, & Tobacco
Fundraising/Development

Government (Federal)
Government (State & Local)

Healthcare Services (For Profit)
Healthcare Services (Nonprofit)
Hospitals
Human Resources/Industrial Relations

Insurance
Insurance (Claims)

Legal Services

Machinery Manufacturing
Management Trainee
Market Research

Network Administration

Paralegal
Pharmaceuticals & Medicine Mfg.
Production (Communications)
Publishing

Real Estate
Religious/Grantmaking/Civic/Professional Orgs.
Reporting
Research (Nontechnical)
Retail/Wholesale Trade

Sales
Scientific Research & Development
Social Assistance
Software Design & Development
Software Publishers

Teaching
Transportation Equipment Mfg.
Transportation Services

Writing/Editing

The starting salaries that go along with each category above range from a high of $50,000 (Transportation Equipment Mfg, / Financial Services) to $12,000 (Agriculture, Forestry, Fishing, Hunting). These data, of course, are raw figures, and they make no account of *where* the graduates were placed—a factor that heavily influences the meaning of a salary—nor whether or not housing and expenses are reflected in the salary. In any case, however, the issue here is that we have 55 separate categories of employment just among the reporting graduates included in the NACE study. These are not vague categories in which English majors *might* work upon graduation; they are actual categories in which English graduates *did* start work in recent years.

A simple Google search under "English Majors" or "English Majors Careers" will also lead to many cataloged lists of job opportunities for English majors—some sites going to the trouble of listing hundreds of separate options. One of my personal favorites is the list of 163 job categories that the English Department at UNC-Chapel Hill posts on the "careers" portion of their website <http://english.unc.edu/undergrad/careers.html>; another is Rutgers University's Career Services page specific for English majors <http://careerservices. rutgers. edu/Menglish.html>, which offers extensive lists of the jobs their recent graduates moved into, as well as a list of jobs in which their experienced alumni work. University of Texas has an exceptionally broad and descriptive list at < http://www.utexas.edu/student/cec/careers/ english.pdf >. Texas has one of the few lists that directs students to such jobs as "intelligence officer" and "Housing and Student Life Coordinator." Knowing, then, that any list of career options will be only a microcosm of the greater possibilities, the following sections briefly detail a few of possibilities available to English majors not identified by the NACE data, areas that attract English majors in remarkable number.

The For-Profit Business Option

Small Business Ownership

As indicated in Chapter One, U.S. Labor Department data show that 56% of English graduates work in private, for-profit business, including a full 14% of them who own their own businesses. One of my former students is part owner of a bakery that specializes in artesian breads, and he continues to pursue his passion for baseball literature. A former English classmate owns his own Washington D.C. consulting firm specializing in telecommunications law. Another started her own bookstore/coffeeshop just outside the entrance of Starved Rock State Park in Utica, Illinois. Along with their specialized skills, these three English majors used their creativity, their interpersonal skills, and their ability to communicate with people to start their own businesses and made a solid go of things.

Many such English majors take over family businesses; others pull together a team of investors or secure a small-business start-up loan. Others work for years and save the investment dollars necessary to own their businesses outright from the start. But the startling fact is that a full 14% of English graduates own their own businesses. That is twice the number of those that work in the non-profit sector of the economy, and I believe it reflects the risk-taking quality so common in English majors, the ability to proceed with an investment not knowing what the final outcome will be.

Publishing

English graduates who have a special talent for editing, along with a genuine personal interest in all aspects of the publishing industry, should indeed pursue an entry-level job in copyediting as a first step in their career path. They should know, too, that the firm they choose does not necessarily have to be the kind of place where they intend to stay for fifty years. The important thing is to learn as much as they can and to contribute as much as they can in their first three to five years. They might work for a trade magazine in the dairy industry or in cabinetry; they might work for a print newspaper or for an on-line magazine. Or they might work for a major publishing house like Random House or Scott, Foresman.

Prospective job applicants would be wise, though, to look at the actual culture and lifestyle of an entry-level copyediting job. The work can be tedious, the pressure can be intense, and for those who live in the big cities where the major publishing houses are, the cost of living can have copyeditors living as they did in college—in a tiny apartment with multiple roommates. But out of that shared experience, along with the friends that first-year editors make, comes a wealth of experience and opportunity on which to build.

That said, I would like to repeat that no one should look at publishing as "The only thing one can do with an English degree besides teach, since all I can do is write." For one thing, why would anyone in the real world of publishing hire someone who thinks that way? Not only is this crudely dismissive of the English skill set, it is even more insulting in its implications about the publishing industry as something someone can do without the critical-thinking skills necessary to *improve* already publishable materials, without the outstanding interpersonal skills necessary to work with authors and co-workers, without the ability to work responsibly under deadline, and without the ability to think creatively and independently about new manuscripts and new ideas.

Publishing is a business, in many ways one like any other business. Likewise, it needs English majors for exactly the same reasons that other businesses need them, not simply because they can tell when a present-participial phrase requires offsetting non-restrictive commas.

The Non-Profit Option

At any time, one can log onto the non-profit job-search site Idealist.org and identify thousands of non-profit job openings around the nation. As I write this, for instance, the site shows 94 full-time openings in the "Art, Architecture, Music" category; in "Human Services" it posts 337 jobs; and in the "Women's Issues" category there are 223 full-time jobs listed. And on top of these three categories, fifty-five others exist. Given the high rate of personal satisfaction that people take in non-profit careers, and given the continual availability of work in this sector of our economy, I remain puzzled as to why only 7% of English majors pursue careers in the non-profits.

Over the past two years, a number of my own students have served as writing and research interns for multiple non-profit agencies near my university. Some did grant-writing and grant-research, others did event planning and management. One of the most impressive accomplishments was an economic impact study of the 46 human-service agencies funded by the local United Way. Two of my English majors, Sarah Heimsoth and Cecilia Reginetz, spent an entire semester culling through the agencies' Form 990 tax documents, from which they determined that these agencies collectively handled over $170,000,000 in total revenue. They also determined how much of that revenue was coming back into the community in such forms as payroll for employees, money for goods and services purchased by the needy, and a great deal of programming that contributes directly to the health and sustainability of the local community, such as after-care, literacy programs, mental-health services, women's shelters, etc.

These English interns put their findings together into a document that also includes narratives of success for each of the 46 agencies, stories that can be used to clarify the importance of each agency, in human terms, to the community. The human service agencies around the country, struggling with the loss of funds with the economic downturn of 2008, need to be able to communicate all the more the importance of what they do. And who better to help in that effort than English majors?

In addition to the "non-profit" jobs identified by search engines like Idealist.org—which include both non-profit businesses and government agencies—many more opportunities exist in large government programs that do not need to advertise positions in traditional search engines. Among these are the Peace Corps, Americorps, and the Foreign Service. To begin a career as a State Department Foreign Service Officer, for instance, the first step is to pass the Foreign Service exam, a test that intently examines a candidate's writing skills, as well as a person's knowledge of culture and politics. The Peace Corps, too, has a very involved application process, which is easily examined from their website at www.peacecorps. gov.

Again, the point in this brief look at the diverse array of job opportunities open to all English majors is to recognize that the question, "What can you do with an English major?" simply cannot be answered in the simple way the question is intended. Such a query typically presupposes that the role of a college major is to serve as vocational training in a specific field of work—a common but narrow vision of college education. Yet even those degrees that some people think of as being "practical" in their connection to the world of business (business management, finance, marketing, accounting) are not simply trade-school degrees, and likewise those graduates can be as under-prepared for an entry-level job as any liberal arts major. Furthermore, many people who graduated with business degrees in their twenties will tell you later on in their careers that is was their liberal arts skills that ultimately accounted for their success, skills they developed not only in their general-education courses in English and History and Foreign Language, but also in their courses in Business, courses which are never taught in a social void, but which also depend heavily on a student's ability to think rationally and to communicate clearly.

Once the job application process is over, and a new graduating class of English majors takes their various places in the work force, a great many of them will still have no clear idea what they ultimately want to do for a living. For some, the choice of jobs will be made primarily for reasons of personal relationship. For others, no one job opportunity will seem any more attractive than any other, and in the end the choice will be made nearly at random. One graduate with a desire to work in for-profit business, for example, might have three job offers simultaneously—one as an administrative assistant at a local cable TV company, another as an entry-level budget coordinator for a big-city bank, and a third as a management trainee for a consumer electronics company—and all three jobs appeal for different reasons. Another graduate with a desire to work in public service might have to choose between a job as an assistant contract negotiator for the Department of Defense or as an assistant analyst with the local Department of Agriculture.

In no way is this uncertainty a bad thing. In the vast majority of cases, the exact nature of an English major's first job matters less than the opportunities the particular job offers to the person to grow into that position—what on-the-job training, what additional education. No one can truly *know* which path to choose, but everyone at some point, for whatever reason, makes the difficult choice and begins his or her individual "apprenticeship" period as a college graduate with a degree in English.

"The Apprenticeship": Five Years of Self Discovery

As I recall, at the age of twenty-two, five years can seem like an eternity, and yet someone who plans to retire at age seventy-two will still have a fifty-year career ahead. The first five years after college is merely an entryway into a long, productive, and rewarding career, and all English majors need to keep this in perspective. Most English majors' first job titles are not necessarily going to impress anyone with their prestige: legal assistant, sales associate, junior analyst, assistant victim's advocate, administrative assistant, assistant grant analyst, research analyst, etc. In addition, English majors can also expect a more humble starting salary than those of their peers who chose more traditionally vocational majors like engineering, accountancy, and finance. Here again, Robyne Hart's metaphor of the tortoise and the hare has important bearing. English majors, like all liberal arts majors, start the "race" of their career slower than do some Business majors, but as the demands of work increase in their complexity and their level of responsibility, English majors accelerate their success by virtue of those aspects of their education and background that prepared them for managerial work—work that primarily consists of reading reports, negotiating face-to-face with audiences of all kinds, making critical decisions, and issuing those decisions in written directive, often in the form of speeches, letters, memos, and reports.

This is not to say that all English majors want to be racing tortoises. But for those who look forward to advancing in a career area of their own choosing, they should look for an entry-level position that meets the following important criteria:

- It offers the "apprentice" valuable training and education
- It requires that the English skills set be used in some productive way
- It breeds pride and satisfaction in the work accomplished
- It involves increasing levels of responsibility and accomplishment over time.

English majors should not see their education simply as a body of knowledge about the books and articles they have read, nor should they consider their first job simply a set of tasks that they perform. An entry-level job is an educational experience that prepares an English major to move on, either within that same company or toward another, and so they need to look for jobs in which they will be enthusiastic about what they will be learning (as they were when they chose English as a major), and just as important, they need to be confident that their English-major skills will allow them to excel.

Examples of Apprenticeships

The following stories of apprenticeship come from the experiences of three former students of mine. I asked these alumni to share their early work histories because of the profound disparity between their career choices. I purposefully chose *not* to illustrate career paths in the "writing-heavy" areas of publishing, marketing, and public relations because such narratives are already available in other books that strictly focus on how English majors find work. What we need to understand much better is the eclectic mix of what most English grads truly do for a living.

The Road to International Business: Lynette Villalobos (Class of 2006)

Lynette Villalobos took my senior project course in the spring of 2006, when her key ambition was to go on for a Ph.D. in English. Three weeks into the course, however, when she learned how few Ph.D.s secure tenure-line positions and how low their salaries are, she changed the focus of her project to overseas job opportunities in private business, non-profit business, and government work. This had been her original plan as a freshman, when she chose English rather than International Studies as her major at Bradley.

After graduation, she received an invitation to live in Prague, the capital of the Czech Republic, and she seized that opportunity by making all the necessary arrangements for a work visa and moving there, with only a vague hope that she could find work once she had settled in. This illustrates the comfort level with uncertainty that English majors have to develop, in that they are rarely sure what they will do next until they actually do it.

Once she arrived in country, Lynette discovered that most of the available jobs required fluency in Czech, but that indeed there were jobs available that could take advantage of her bi-lingual skills in both English and Spanish. The first job she took was a short-term "dual diligence" project with GE Money Bank. This international banking institution was in the process of acquiring a bank in Colombia, and they hired Lynette as a researcher. Her role was to conduct all primary and secondary research on Colombia's economic status and to compile all the statistical findings that would provide information on the risks and opportunities of acquiring the bank. At the end of the project, Lynette reported all results, with a detailed conclusion, and presented it to the head of the Risk Department. "I was a bit ambivalent about my report," Lynette says, "as I was an English and Psychology double major, neither of which had anything directly to do with economics or risk assessment. Nevertheless, I was confident in my strong analytical skills and in my ability to carry out the extensive research." The bank was very pleased with the results of her work.

Once that project concluded, Lynette went right back on the market, and she applied for a sales position with Marcus Evans—not because she was attracted to sales, per se, but because she was impressed with the 64-country reach of Marcus Evans's business operations. As it turned out, the sales position was a permanent ad, due to the heavy turnover in that area, and when the HR department looked over Lynette's résumé, they offered her a job as a "Conference Producer." When such positions are advertised in the United States, they are often referred to under the general heading of "Event Planning."

Here again is a perfect example of the way in which opportunities present themselves to English majors over time. Lynette did not go to college to become a Conference Producer in the Czech Republic; her communication and interpersonal skills (and her willingness to take risks) brought the unforeseeable opportunity to the surface, and she jumped at it. It was the fruit not only of her marketable skills, but also of her self-confidence.

Lynette began her work in October of 2006. As a Conference Producer (CP) for the Retail Finance Division, she was responsible for organizing conferences for this sector of the company. For the first six months, her director would provide her with the general topics, and then she would develop the conference agenda and secure top speakers on the subjects. The role of a CP also includes managing the event on-site, as well as delivering the opening and closing conference remarks.

After five months on the job, Lynette told her manager that she wanted to try to develop her own topics independently and to carry out all the preliminary research herself, and she was immediately given that authority. Her first completely independent event was on Mobile Payments, a topic that excited her after reading an article on the subject in *The Economist*. After testing the topic with leaders in the field, Lynette decided to go ahead and organize the event. Business leaders from all over Europe, North America, Africa, and the Middle East came together in Stockholm, Sweden, to listen to speakers and to discuss the latest case studies in the field of payments. "This event was especially significant for me," Lynette remarks, "because I was fully responsible for it, from the very idea to the final execution of the event."

Because of her demonstrated ability to meet deadlines and to develop her own conferences topics on a continuous basis, Lynette was then promoted to Senior Conference Producer, with management responsibility throughout the production process. That process itself merits a close examination, in that it so clearly draws on the native skills of any successful English major (reading, interpersonal communication, audience analysis, writing, and creative thinking):

Stage 1: The Development of Conference Topics

The first step in Lynette's work required her to use her research and reading skills to stay current with the topics in her industry that would merit business leaders to gather for an international conference. Marcus Evans was producing a new conference every twenty-five working days, for a total of eight major conferences a year, so this had to be a continual process of reading and creative analysis to identify those potential topics that would prove lucrative.

Stage 2: Generating an Agenda

After a topic had been identified and decided upon, Lynette interacted by telephone with leaders in the chosen industry to identify potential sub-topics for the event, as well as any special challenges that might cause difficulty. After a great many interpersonal contacts with senior industry experts, she eventually had enough information to write a comprehensive conference agenda. The agenda itself was, logically, one of the principle tools used to market the conference throughout Europe and beyond, so the content itself, as well as the descriptive language had to appeal to the targeted audience. Lynette needed to understand her audience well enough to know the right number of topics and the appropriate choice of issues or case studies to cover a two-day event.

Stage 3: Producing the Event

After writing and distributing the agenda, Lynette then had to secure the speakers for the event. The production cycle begins approximately four months prior to the actual conference date, and acquiring speakers was never easy. Every Marcus Evans conference producer is tasked with trying to secure the best participating companies and sixteen of the most prominent speakers in the field. Once the participants are finalized, the CP briefs the sales, marketing, and sponsorship departments individually on the event so that each internal department understands what it is they are selling. These departments then promote the conference throughout Europe and the Middle East. While promotion proceeds, the conference producer is responsible for identifying vendors and potential sponsors for each event — in essence, for identifying the commercial angles of the event and working closely with the entire sponsorship team to write the actual promotional materials (e.g. conference agenda, press releases, e-newsletters, and event website). Finally, the conference producer acts as the public face of Marcus Evans at the conference, giving the opening and closing remarks at the event and serving as the on-site manager to ensure that the event runs smoothly.

In two years, Lynette Villalobos accomplished all of this, in a foreign country whose native language she did not know. With that experience behind her, she then returned to America to pursue a Masters degree in Integrated Marketing Communications from the Medill School of Journalism at Northwestern University. Her goal in pursuing this particular graduate program was to become an international marketing professional and continue working in a multinational context.

With her degree now in hand, Lynette has been working as an Analyst in the Marketplace Analytics department of Havi Global Solutions since February of 2010. In her new position, she works on producing and distributing marketing and supply chain reports that help manage and track national promotions for a major national restaurant chain. Specifically, she is responsible for managing report quality, conducting sales data analysis, understanding business trends, and contributing to key report highlights.

Like her work in the Czech Republic, Lynette's new position feeds her need to grow continually in her knowledge of current business challenges, and it draws upon all her communication skills, both written and oral. Furthermore, she routinely collaborates with people in many interdependent departments. Her own account of her work emphasizes the importance of the skills that she worked so hard to develop in her years as an English major:

> My new job requires me to have a holistic understanding of the businesses I work for, to be detailed oriented, and to be able to switch constantly between the "hard" and "soft" aspects of business and marketing. I absolutely love being able to dig through data, but I also like to step back and look at the big picture. I definitely believe that having been an English major has taught me to look at the story, not just the data, to find and interpret the key message, and always to think about my audience.

The Take-Off Period

Once English majors have completed their apprenticeship period, having learned and applied a new set of skills, they are then in an especially strong position, in that they have further honed the skills they began to develop as English majors—skills that can never be completely mastered—and they have also established themselves as valuable experts in a particular industry. For some English graduates, this happens quickly; for others, it is a protracted process of finding the right "fit." Regardless how long the apprenticeship period takes, every non-teaching English major at some point finds him or herself an expert in some field. After months of searching, I have found no long- or short-term studies of English majors' career paths, and so all anyone has to go on is the representative experience of those English majors we know and those whose careers have brought them fame (see chapter 9). Certainly, the experiences of the following former students of mine speak to the reality of what I refer to as the "take-off period" between the low-paying/high-training world of entry-level work and the higher-paying/high-expertise world of a leader in any industry. The model that comes down to us from the medieval craft guilds of Apprentice, Journeyman, and

Master works well to describe the stages that English majors move through as they advance in their careers.

Examples of "Journeyman" Experience

The Road to Information Technology: Amy Courtney (Class of 2000)

Amy Courtney, another Bradley English graduate, is today an IT business analyst in a Fortune-50 insurance company's Systems Department, that department being one of the largest IT "shops" in the country.

In her first six years after graduation, Amy worked for a number of small business owners in a wide range of enterprises. In two of her positions, in particular, the firms' owners had challenges in their businesses for which they turned to Amy for especially creative technology solutions. In the first of these, Amy worked for a distributor of industrial equipment and controls. As one of her first key projects for that employer, she received training in the technical area that would define her career path in the coming years. Her assignment was to master a specialized software product specifically for distributors of all kinds, a program that integrates warehouse/inventory management, accounting, purchasing, and sales. The software company itself trained her over a period of months, not only through one-on-one contact with the company's employees, but also through two formal classes with the company: one in system administration (all the servers and technical support systems that allow a computer terminal to function) and another in a technology that allows a database to be accessed for the purpose of creating managerial reports, not only about what happened in the company's operations, but why and how they happened that way.

This training in software operations and its application to an actual business was Amy's first step in her growth as an Information-Technology professional. Another large step came in her second position as the vice-president of a start-up small business. She was hired by a woman who had a creative business plan and who had secured funding to create a nationwide advertising source for the magazine industry, in both print and electronic format. The business owner's role was primarily in interpersonal, face-to-face sales, and Amy's role was to establish the business operations at home from the ground up. She helped create the company's e-commerce site and served as the liaison between the company owner and the web development team hired to develop the website. Her role in that project was largely to translate the owner's vision for the website (known as business requirements in the IT world) into technical requirements (specifications) that the web development team could follow to build the website. In this role, as in her earlier position, Amy learned that business and IT speak two different languages, and she learned to be fluent in both. Amy summarizes her professional multi-lingualism this way: "In my work, I have to shape messages to the executives I work for in one way. With my fellow IT people I speak a very different language, and I write a different way again for my firm's business partners."

The next step in Amy's career was a move from small business into the field of IT training. In that work, among her many projects, she developed an entire curriculum in the specialized area of business-intelligence technology. Once that initial step was complete, she then became a key player on a team that developed the actual classes for the IT and business professionals who would be using this technology. To develop effective materials, she spoke to learners face-to-face to determine exactly what their level of knowledge was, and then she crafted her instructions in words appropriate to each of her audiences, often demonstrating the instructions with visual rhetoric as well. She worked in this area for two years, and then her success in the business-intelligence curriculum project led to a new job opportunity as a business analyst (albeit a very technically savvy one).

In all her work—whether in her first two apprenticeship positions, or in her later IT roles—Amy "learned how to learn" computer applications and technology, and she learned the specialized knowledge and language of each area of business, most importantly, the nature and the function of accounting. In order, then, to apply this knowledge practically, she drew upon some of her key skills as an English major: her ability to read and analyze complex texts, her ability to tailor messages to the needs of diverse audiences, and her ability to put herself in the shoes of the various groups and individuals that she serves. On that last point, Amy speaks to the importance of a business leader's ability to understand people: "When it comes to empathy, you are not just using it when you are writing, you use it when you are doing everything, in every interaction you have with other people, with people who work for you, with people on your team, with management, with everyone." Having now begun her M.B.A. program at Indiana University's Kelley School of Business, Amy is still "doing English," but the texts that she reads and creates are far afield from the Margaret Atwood, Ray Bradbury, and George Orwell novels of her college years.

The Road to Consultancy: Jennifer Flunker (Class of 1995)

Most people have no idea what the term "consultancy" actually means. We know, however, that you cannot major in it in college, and we also know that English majors often go this route, at some point, after graduation. Consultancy as a profession is a business-service industry that offers expert advice (consultation) to companies who are seeking to improve their operations in some way. They offer consultative advice, for a fee, in every imaginable segment in the life of a business: management, technical and computer operations, logistics, human resources, health and retirement benefits, information technology, etc. And they succeed so well because for years they have helped companies become more productive, more efficient, and more competitive.

Firms like Accenture (formerly Anderson Consulting), Ernst & Young, Hewitt, and KPMG interview English majors on college campuses every year, sometimes looking to hire writers to be members of consulting teams; sometimes they in fact train English majors to become experts in technical areas besides writing before sending them out into the field as a part of a team. But most people wind up in consultancy in a circuitous route, after working for some years in a particular industry.

For my former student Jennifer Flunker, the winding road into consultancy began with a part-time internship in a small publishing firm while she was a student at Bradley. From her sophomore year through her senior year, she worked for the Spoon River Press, a small press owned by a married couple who specialized in print catalogues. Mentored by both owners, Jennifer learned every aspect of a small publishing business—from copyediting, to packaging and mailing, to bookkeeping—and after she graduated from Bradley with her English degree, she stayed on at Spoon River for a year as a full-time employee.

Building on her four years of small-press publishing experience, Jennifer moved on in 1996 to an entry-level job as an acquisitions editor with the Health Administration Press in Chicago (HAP), a division of the non-profit American College of Healthcare Executives. In her first year at HAP, she spent a great deal of time talking directly with current authors about potential manuscripts, as well as with potential new authors whose research had gained attention in the healthcare industry. In her first weeks in that job, Jennifer made the transition to a formal workplace culture, and once she acquired the necessary wardrobe, she found that she liked the structure and took to the company immediately.

In 1997, she was promoted to Editor in the "Editorial and Production" division of Health Administration Press. As an employee benefit, she was also offered tuition support to pursue any higher-education degree program she desired, and she decided to begin an M.B.A. program at Loyola University Chicago. During the next two and a half years, Jennifer worked full-time during the day and took two evening graduate courses per quarter, graduating with her degree in May of 1999. "I had so much fun in my M.B.A. work," she says, "because with all my work experience, I was able to apply all the things I was learning, like in-house inventory and logistics (you need to know where all your stuff is). Most of the learning was very logical and practical, and I liked the learning that helped me make an immediate difference back at my job."

Another important element of Jennifer's M.B.A. program was an international summer course, the Economics of International Business, taught at Loyola's campus in Rome, Italy. In the summer of 1998, Italy was preparing for the currency conversion to the Euro, and the students were able to see how economic principles were playing out in the daily life of Italian consumers. Between forty and fifty students lived together in dormitories owned by Loyola, and once the program was over, Jennifer remained friends with many of them, traveling together in the summer for years afterwards.

In the course of her M.B.A. program, Jennifer had always found the finance and economics courses the most challenging, but when the Chief Financial Officer of the American College of Healthcare Executives asked her how her M.B.A. was going, she told him the finance courses were rough, and he offered to tutor her in the relevant financial skills on lunch hours. Once she got through the basics, she was fine, and ever since then she has counseled any humanities major in business *not* to be afraid to ask for help.

The M.B.A. program as a whole filled in the blanks in Jennifer's education relative to her work in the business of publishing, especially in terms of the specialized language of business. While she was still an editor at Health Administration Press, she had begun to be able to translate the technical language of specific business operations for audiences of executive decision makers, a skill that would take her far in the coming years.

In 1999, with her M.B.A. in hand, Jennifer was contacted by one of her friends from the summer course in Italy. Her friend had just interviewed for a job with one of "The Big Four" accounting and consulting firms in America, Ernst & Young, and she had realized while interviewing that she was not right for the job, but that Jennifer would be perfect. So Jennifer contacted the company, interviewed, and was offered the job within three days. This is exactly what the career experts mean when they tell young people coming out of college that networking is a vital part of the job-search process in the real world of work. Someone who knew Jennifer's education, talents, experience, and personality let her know of the possibility. Jennifer saw the duck—as Dick Moy, the founding Dean of SIU Medical School, expressed it in Chapter 1—and she grabbed it. Coincidentally, it had been Jennifer, as President of the English Honors Society, who had hosted Dick Moy on the Bradley campus in 1994.

In her first financial job after six years in publishing, Jennifer worked at Ernst & Young as a "Communications Pursuit Specialist." In this position, she worked as a member of a series of four-person teams to put together proposals and credentials that a lead sales person would present to current and potential clients. Ernst & Young is one of the four biggest firms specializing in independent external financial audits, something that every public company is required to go through annually by the Securities Exchange Commission. Thus, over the course of the next year and a half, Jennifer developed a great deal of expertise communicating complex issues of accountancy in terms that could be understood by a variety of different executive audiences. In her new line of work, that team effort to draw new business to the firm was commonly referred to as "pursuit."

After a year and a half in her original pursuit role, Jennifer moved to the Dallas office of Ernst & Young and took on a greater leadership role as the Project Manager on a new team serving the needs of a series of global clients. This time, the service that they were selling to Ernst & Young clients was "expatriate administration." Simply put, they managed the administrative needs of American companies overseas: their housing contracts, their benefits and healthcare packages, their telecommunications systems, their computer operations, their families' educational needs. Such work is, in Jennifer's words, "an amazingly complex human reality." Whenever problems arose—and problems are especially difficult when they are international—Jennifer's team would sometimes be the client's only English-speaking contact, and whenever any client would contact her team, Ernst & Young would always have the infrastructure in place to support the client's needs.

During this part of her development as a consultant, Jennifer's team focused on only a handful of clients in London, Helsinki, and New York, and they would travel to the key sites regularly. Time on site would vary, but it would typically be 1-2 weeks, then home for awhile, and then back again for a few weeks. From 2000 through 2004, Jennifer was away from home more than in her home.

Not everyone is cut out for this type of international consultancy. It is a high-energy, all-consuming style of work, and while the consultants are in the midst of project, daily life is routinely intense. Jennifer found it especially beneficial, however, because every single day was filled with constant learning. "I had enough structure," she says, "to keep things sane, but every day came with new challenges and new problems to solve."

After four full years of heavy travel, Jennifer was ready to find a job that would keep her at home much more, and so in 2004, she took a job with another of the "Big Four" consulting firms, PricewaterhouseCoopers. Her new title at PwC is "Client Driver Leader."

Jennifer describes her job as "a behind-the-scenes traffic cop." She is the primary point of contact for an expanded team of people around the world who serve one account that includes more than 120 people, all of whom know that she is the person to go to with questions and problems. She keeps track of everything involved in that client's account management needs. Thus as a "Client Driver," she steers people to the knowledge that they need to increase their efficiency at whatever area of business they are in.

In addition to her account responsibilities, Jennifer also serves as a coach for her team. Six people report directly to Jennifer, and they look to her for guidance on how to communicate with their partners—where to look for client research, for instance, or where to find a particular subject-matter expert within the firm. In her work as a Client Driver Leader, Jennifer is also a teacher, with key roles to play in the sharing of knowledge. For Example, Jennifer co-developed and led a national webcast for client drivers on "Being Efficient." And in the industry more generally, Jennifer is a member of a leadership council that serves as a resource for client drivers everywhere to share best practices. In all of her work now, Jennifer is in a key knowledge-sharing role, either with her company's external clients or with her own internal constituencies. She is a professional communicator of specialized knowledge in business services, managing all of those communications herself as she tailors information to the needs of a multitude of complex audiences.

Having been schooled at Bradley in Jack Stillinger's "Huh? Oh Yeah? So What?" approach to essay writing, Jennifer has adapted that paradigm over the years to the countless times she taught teams of people to communicate with executive audiences:

> In my work as a consultant, we feature first the "Huh?" question. This is the services that we are offering to our clients, whatever they might be. Then we move right to the "So What," which to my clients means "What is the value to my company, and what will be the return on our investment?" The "Oh Yeah?" question rarely comes into play at my level, but it always has to be there, and that can be found in the supporting documentation. I leave that to the CPAs.

Like so many other successful English majors, Jennifer translates and applies in her workplace the same skills she used in her college English classrooms. She reads challenging material, she listens to people, she analyzes what she reads and hears, and she shares her analysis in constructive ways. She "does English" in her workplace every day.

Jennifer Flunker's career path demonstrates very dramatically how the early stages of learning after college—what I am calling the Apprenticeship Period—can begin in the simplest of internship experiences. In her first position in publishing, for example, Jennifer spent a great deal of time packing catalogues into boxes and mailing them off.

We should remember here the humble beginnings of many of the most prominent business leaders in America—James McNerney, for instance, began his career in 1975 (with a B.A. in the liberal-arts field of American Studies) as a "brand manager" for Downy Fabric Softener with the Proctor & Gamble Company, working for some years marketing Coast and Bounce. By 2005, after having risen to higher and higher positions for both G.E. and 3M, McNerney was named CEO of Boeing, the largest jet airline and military aircraft manufacturer in the world, with assets over 61 billion dollars. Likewise, Aylwin Lewis, as we saw in

Chapter 1, worked the counter at Jack-in-the-Box before moving on to his amazing success in the retail and restaurant industries. The important issue for a motivated undergraduate is to find a position where the student can show that he or she is capable of being trained in new areas of learning. The skills of the English major then can be transferred and applied in constructive, important ways, regardless the nature of the work. Jennifer Flunker did not major in Consultancy with a minor in Client-Driver Studies; she majored in English.

CHAPTER 9:
An English Major Hall of Fame

In his beautiful "Elegy Written in a Country Churchyard," the 18th-century poet Thomas Gray glorifies the dignity of farm laborers long forgotten, reminding his 21st-century readers that fame has nothing to do with virtue, wisdom, or human worth, reminding us in perpetuity that "The paths of glory lead but to the grave." English majors, however, for the most part, need no such reminder. Almost no one chooses to major in English to pursue fame and glory, any more than they do to pursue high salaries. Nevertheless, in large numbers, English majors have left lasting marks in public service, in business, in medicine, in sports, and in the creative arts. As this book has emphasized from the outset, an English major is free to pursue his or her passion in any career field, and even within the narrow limits of what constitutes "celebrity" in American culture, many former English majors achieved so much in their chosen profession that they are properly recognized not as journeymen, but as "master" English majors.

Some of the names on my "Hall of Fame" list were originally compiled by the English Department at Mississippi State University (see www.msstate.edu/dept/English/ ENCelebs.html), and that list now appears on many English Department websites around the country—Drake, Rutgers, Hancock College, Central Washington University, UC-Bakersfield, and others. I uncovered the degree information for the rest of them primarily by digging through biographies, but some information—like Supreme Court Justice Abe Fortas's undergraduate major—required assistance from college alumni offices and reference librarians. Often, if an accomplished humanities major does have a biography that features business or public service, the biographers do not see how English, or History, or Philosophy are relevant to that person's success, and so the college major goes unmentioned, only the college is identified. I am especially indebted to the research professionals at Princeton University's Firestone Library, Bradley University's Cullom-Davis Library, and at the University of Illinois at Urbana-Champaign for their assistance in locating that information—and most especially to Laura Tatum, Archivist at the Yale University Library, who was herself, not surprisingly, an undergraduate English major.

For the sake of brevity, I have excluded almost all the second (or third) undergraduate degrees that these people completed in addition to their work in English.

A
(HIGHLY INCOMPLETE)
ENGLISH MAJOR'S HALL OF FAME

I begin with the creative writers in a special place of honor because they all chose to devote the vast majority of their professional energies to producing the literature that allows us to examine and engage our own culture. Their work entertains us and brings us together and gives everyone that same chance to grow in empathy and human insight that it gives to English majors. Without such people, the discipline of English could look only backwards.

Fiction Writers:

Douglas Adams (*Hitchhiker's Guide to the Galaxy*)
    B.A. English, Cambridge University, 1974
William Peter Blatty (*The Exorcist, The Ninth Configuration*)
    B.A. English, Georgetown University, 1950; M.A. Georgetown, 1954
Willa Cather (*O Pioneers!, My Antonia*; 1923 Pulitzer for *One of Ours*)
    A.B. English Composition and English Literature, University of Nebraska, 1895
Tom Clancy (*Hunt for Red October*, co-owner Baltimore Orioles baseball team)
    B.A. English, Loyola College, Baltimore, 1968
Philip José Farmer (*The Lovers, River World*; Hugo-Award Winner 1953, 1968, 1972)
    B.A. English, Bradley University, 1950
Joseph Heller (*Catch 22*)
    Undergraduate English USC, NYU; M.A. Columbia University 1949
John Irving (*World According to Garp, Cider House Rules*)
    B.A. English, University of New Hampshire, 1965
Edward P. Jones (*Lost in the City*; 2004 Pulitzer Prize for *The Known World*)
    B.A. English, Holy Cross, 1972; M.F.A., University of Virginia, 1981
Stephen King (*Carrie, The Shining*)
    English major, University of Maine at Orono, 1966-1970
Madeleine L'Engle (*A Wrinkle in Time, A Ring of Endless Light*)
    B.A. English, Smith College, 1941
Larry McMurtry (1986 Pulitzer Prize for *Lonesome Dove*)
    B.A. English, University of North Texas, 1958

Toni Morrison (*Beloved*, Nobel Prize for Literature 1993)
  B.A. English, Howard University 1953; M.A., Cornell University, 1955
Joyce Carol Oates (*them*, "Where Are You Going, Where Have You Been?")
  B.A. English, Syracuse University 1960; M.A. University Wisconsin, 1961
Philip Roth (*Good-Bye Columbus*)
  B.A. English, Bucknell University, 1954; M.A., University of Chicago, 1955
Amy Tan (*The Joy Luck Club*)
  B.A. English, San Jose State University, 1973
John Updike (The *Rabbit* series)
  B.A. English, Harvard University, 1954
Eudora Welty (*A Curtain Green, The Optimist's Daughter*)
  B.A. English, University of Wisconsin, 1929

Poets:

Gwendolyn Brooks (1950 Pulitzer Prize for *Annie Allen*)
  English major, Kennedy King College, 1936.
Billy Collins (U.S. Poet Laureate 2001-2003; *Questions About Angels*)
  B.A. English, Holy Cross, 1963; Ph.D. University of California at Riverside
Countee Cullen (*Color, Copper Sun, The Black Christ and Other Poems*)
  B.A. English, New York University, 1925; M.A. English, Harvard, 1926
Rita Dove (U.S. Poet Laureate 1993-95, 1987 Pulitzer Prize for *Thomas and Beulah*)
  B.A. English, Miami University, 1973; M.F.A. University of Iowa, 1977
Carolyn Forché (*The Country Between Us, The Angel of History*)
  B.A. Creative Writing, Michigan State University, 1972
Allen Ginsberg (*Howl and Other Poems*)
  B.A. English, Columbia University, 1949
W.S. Merwin (1970 Pulitzer Prize for *The Carrier of Ladders*)
  B.A. English, Princeton University, 1948
Robert Pinsky (U.S. Poet Laureate 1997-2000, *The Inferno of Dante*)
  B.A. English, Rutgers University, 1962; Ph.D. Stanford, 1968
Sylvia Plath (*Ariel*, 1982 Pulitzer Prize for *The Collected Poems*)
  B.A. English, Smith College, 1955
Adrienne Rich (*Diving into the Wreck*)
  B.A. English, Radcliffe, 1951
Dr. Seuss a.k.a Theodor Geisel (*Green Eggs and Ham*)
  B.A. English, Dartmouth, 1925
Charles Simic (U.S. Poet Laureate 2007- ; 1990 Pulitzer for *The World Doesn't End*)
  B.A. English, New York University, 1966
James Wright (1972 Pulitzer Prize for *Collected Poems*)
  B.A. English, Kenyon College, 1951; Ph.D. University of Washington, 1959

Dramatists and Screenwriters:

Much more so than poetry or fiction, drama is a performance art. And since drama is tied so intimately to the business of theater production, many great American playwrights leave college long before graduation to pursue their craft in the world of the playhouse rather than the classroom. **Lorraine Hansberry**, **Lillian Hellman**, **Eugene O'Neill**, **Sam Shepard**, **Neil Simon**, **Thornton Wilder**, **Tennessee Williams** for instance, all left college without completing a degree and began practicing their craft directly.

August Wilson left *high school* (angry over a charge of plagiarism) and studied on his own at the Carnegie Library, where they issued him a degree of their own creation, the only such degree ever issued. **Edward Albee** was expelled from Trinity College in Connecticut for ditching classes.

Hence, the following ranks of actual English-degree holders has been thinned from what it might have been:

Tony Kushner (1993 Pulitzer Prize for *Angels in America*)
    B.A. English, Columbia University 1978
Archibald MacLeish (1959 Pulitzer Prize and Tony Award for *J.B.*)
    B.A. English, Yale University, 1915
David Mamet (1984 Pulitzer Prize for *Glengarry Glen Ross*)
    B.A. Literature, Goddard College, 1969
Arthur Miller (*The Crucible*, 1949 Pulitzer Prize for *Death of a Salesman*)
    B.A. English, University of Michigan, 1938
Wendy Wasserstein (1989 Pulitzer Prize and Tony Award for *The Heidi Chronicles*)
    M.A. Creative Writing, City College of New York, 1971

Songwriters:

As with the playwrights listed above, many successful songwriters never attended college or left after a few months to pursue their success as performing lyricists. I include Don Henley below because of his public recognition of the importance of his two years of literary studies at North Texas State, which introduced him to Thoreau's and Emerson's views on God in nature, something that helped him cope with the illness and early death of his father. Henley would go on to found the "Walden Woods Project" in 1989, which increased the protected area of the ecosystem at Walden from 60 to 90% of the full 2,680 acres.

Leonard Cohen ("Bird on a Wire," "Hallelujah," "Suzanne")
    B.A. English, McGill University, 1955
Don Henley (with Glen Frey: "Hotel California," "Witchy Woman," "Dirty Laundry")
    English major, North Texas State University, 1968-69
Chris Isaak ("Baby Did a Bad, Bad Thing," *The Chris Isaak Show*)
    B.A. English, University of the Pacific, 1980
Kris Kristofferson ("Me and Bobby McGee," "Help Me Make It Through the Night")
    B.A. Creative Writing, Pomona College, 1958; M.A. English, Oxford, 1960

Bobby Lopez (*Avenue Q*)
    B.A. English, Yale University, 1997
Colin Meloy (The Decemberists — "O Valencia")
    B.A. Creative Writing, University of Montana, 1998
Randy Owen (Lead singer for Alabama — "Feels So Right" and "Tennessee River")
    B.A. English, Jacksonville State University, 1973
Corinne Bailey Rae ("Like a Star," "Put Your Records On")
    B.A. English, University of Leeds, 2000
Amy Ray (Indigo Girls — "Closer to Fine," "Hammer and Nail")
    B.A. English, Emory University, 1986
Emily Saliers (Indigo Girls. See above)
    B.A. English, Emory University, 1985
Paul Simon ("Bridge over Troubled Water," "Sounds of Silence," *Graceland*)
    B.A. English, Queens College, 1963

Non-Fiction Writers

This amorphous category of writers is so broad, that it is difficult to decide whether any given writer belongs here or in another category, since many essayist and biographers, many nature writers and scholars, also achieved great things as novelists, journalists, or screenwriters.

A few of them, as we have seen in other categories, were English majors for awhile and then changed majors. **John Gardner**, for instance, was a Stanford English major from 1930-33, but he took a year off to try his hand as a novelist. When he did not succeed as he had hoped, he returned to Stanford as a Psychology major. In the coming years, he went on to become President Johnson's Secretary of HEW and to publish many books with his creative ideas about social and political issues, the last being *On Leadership* (1990).

Joseph Campbell (*The Power of Myth, The Hero of a Thousand Faces*)
    B.A. English Literature, Columbia University, 1925
Ernestine Gilbreth Carey (*Cheaper by the Dozen, Belles on Their Toes*)
    B.A. English, Smith College, 1929
Garrison Keillor (Radio Personality, *A Prairie Home Companion*)
    B.A. English, University of Minnesota, 1966
Hellen Keller (*The Story of My Life, The World I Live In, Light in My Darkness*)
    B.A. English, Radcliffe College, 1904
Sam Tanenhaus (Editor, *New York Times Book Review*)
    B.A. English, Grinnell College, 1977; M.A. English Literature, Yale, 1978
Naomi Wolf (*The Beauty Myth*)
    B.A. English, Yale, 1984; Rhodes Scholar 1985-87

Actors:

Like the creative writers, many gifted English majors who are drawn to the uncertain world of acting leave college for various reasons. Success drew Matt Damon away from Harvard just before graduation; for different reasons, Harrison Ford left Ripon College at the last possible minute. Vin Diesel left after three years to pursue his dreams as a screenwriter, and David Duchovny left Yale having completed all but the thesis for his Ph.D. in English. **Heather Graham** left her studies in English at UCLA after only two years, having already experienced success in *Drugstore Cowboy* (1989); Academy-Award winner **Reese Wither- spoon** left Stanford after only one year as an English major.

The relationship between English and acting makes perfect sense when we consider that the craft entails 1) the internalization of a written script and 2) the empathetic ability not only to understand another person, but for a time to be that person for an audience.

Alan Alda (*M*A*S*H*)
    B.S. English, Fordham University, 1956
Ed Burns (*Saving Private Ryan*; writer-director *The Brothers McMullen*)
    B.A. English, Hunter College, 1992
Chevy Chase (*Saturday Night Live, Caddyshack*)
    B.A. English, Bard College, 1967
Bradley Cooper (*Alias, He's Just Not That Into You, Wedding Crashers*)
    B.A. English, Georgetown University, 1997
Matt Damon (*Bourne Identity,* Academy Award for Best Screenplay *Good Will Hunting*)
    English Major, Harvard University, 1988-1992
Vin Diesel (*xXx, Fast and the Furious*; writer-director *Strays, Multi-Facial*)
    English Major, Hunter College, 1985-87
David Duchovny (*The X-Files*)
    B.A. English, Princeton, 1982; M.A. English, Yale University 1987
Harrison Ford (*Star Wars, Raiders of the Lost Ark, Witness*)
    English Major, Ripon College, 1961-64
Jodi Foster (Academy Award Best Actress *Silence of the Lambs*)
    B.A. English, Yale University, 1985
Bonnie Franklin (*One Day at a Time*)
    B.A. English, UCLA, 1966
Hugh Grant (*Notting Hill, Four Weddings and a Funeral*)
    B.A. English, Oxford University, 1982
Famke Janssen (*X-Men, Goldeneye*)
    M.A. English, Columbia University, 1992
Tommy Lee Jones (*Men in Black*; Academy Awards for *The Fugitive* and JFK)
    B.A. English, Harvard University, 1969
Catherine Keener (*Being John Malkovich, Capote*)
    B.A. English, Wheaton College, 1983
Paul Newman (*Cool Hand Luke*; Academy Award Best Actor for *The Color of Money*)
    B.A. English, Kenyon College, 1949
David Hyde Pierce (Multiple Emmy Awards for *Frasier*)
    B.A. English, Yale University, 1981

Chris Pine (*Star Trek*)
    B.A. English, Berkeley, 2002
Julia Stiles (*Save the Last Dance, The Bourne Ultimatum*)
    B.A. English, Columbia University, 1985
Christopher Reeve (*Superman, Somewhere in Time*)
    B.A. English, Cornell University, 1974
George C. Scott (Academy Award Best Actor for *Patton*)
    B.A. English, University of Missouri, 1953
Emma Thompson (Academy Award Best Actress for *Howard's End*)
    B.A. English, Cambridge University, 1980
Sigourney Weaver (*Alien, Ghostbusters, The Year of Living Dangerously*)
    B.A. English, Stanford University, 1971
Renée Zellweger (Academy Award Best Actress for *Cold Mountain*)
    B.A. English, University of Texas at Austin, 1992

Talk-Show Hosts:

It should seem obvious by now why English majors would succeed as talk-show hosts, given that the entire point of the enterprise is to engage in witty conversation that genuinely interests and entertains a broad audience. Whereas David Letterman and Oprah were communications majors, and though Jay Leno did his undergraduate degree in Speech Pathology at Emerson College, the following English majors also have done fairly well in their high-profile career paths.

Johnny Carson (Host, *The Tonight Show*)
    B.A. English, University of Nebraska, 1949
Dick Cavett (Host, *The Dick Cavett Show*)
    B.A. English, Yale University, 1958
Mary Hart (Co-host, *Entertainment Tonight*)
    B.A. English, Augustana College SD, 1969
Bill Maher (Host, *Politically Incorrect*)
    B.A. English, Cornell University, 1978
Conan O'Brien (Host, *The Tonight Show*; President, *Harvard Lampoon*)
    B.A. Literature, Harvard University, 1985
Joan Rivers (Comedienne, Actress, and Talk-Show Host)
    B.A. English, Barnard College, 1958
Barbara Walters (Host *20/20* and *The View*)
    B.A. English, Sarah Lawrence University, 1953

Film Directors and Producers:

Film-making, too, draws English majors, but even more so than playwriting or screenwriting, directing draws people away from college as soon as the first opportunity comes to make a film. Film mogul **Steven Spielberg** (*E.T., The Color Purple, Schindler's*

List) left his English studies at the University of California at Long Beach in 1969 (completing a UCLB degree in 2002 in Film Production and Electric Arts); **Sam Raimi** (*Spiderman I, II, III*) left his English program at Michigan State after three semesters. The director of *Clerks*, **Kevin Smith**, left his Creative Writing studies at New Jersey's New School for Social Research after a notorious water-balloon incident. And **Paul Thomas Anderson** (*Boogie Nights, Magnolia*) was an English major at Emerson College for only two semesters before he left to pursue film. That leaves the following ever-growing list of amazingly accomplished English-major film-makers:

John Frankenheimer (*Manchurian Candidate, Birdman of Alcatraz*)
> B.A. English, Williams College, 1951

Jim Jarmusch (*Stranger than Paradise, Down by Law*)
> B.A. English Columbia University, 1975

Neil Jordan (*Michael Collins, The Crying Game, Mona Lisa*)
> B.A. Irish Literature and History, University College Dublin, 1972

Elia Kazan (*On the Waterfront, East of Eden, Splendor in the Grass*)
> B.A. English, Williams College, 1930

Michael Mann (*Collateral, Ali, Last of the Mohicans*)
> B.A. English, University of Wisconsin at Madison, 1965

David O. Russell (*I Heart Huckabees, Three Kings, Flirting with Disaster*)
> B.A. English, Amherst University, 1981

Martin Scorcese (*The Departed, Goodfellas, Raging Bull, Taxi Driver*)
> B.A. English, New York University, 1963

Sam Mendes (*American Beauty, Road to Perdition, Revolutionary Road*)
> B.A. English, Cambridge University, 1987

Sports Figures:

Having poured through a few hundred athletes' biographies, I have determined that English is not a common undergraduate major for well-known athletes. Just as with film-making, songwriting, scriptwriting, and acting, many of the most talented college sports heroes move on to their professional careers before completing college. That said, the following four English-degree holders have risen to very prominent positions in the world of sports.

Bart Giamatti (Baseball Commissioner 1988-89, President of Yale University 1978-86)
> B.A. English, Yale University, 1960; Ph.D. Comparative Literature, Yale, 1964

Joe Paterno (Head Football Coach, Penn State University 1966-present)
> B.A. English, Brown University, 1958

Marty Schottenheimer (Head Coach of Four NFL teams 1984-present)
> B.A. English, University of Pittsburgh, 1965

John Wooden (UCLA Basketball Coach with 10 National Championships)
> B.A. English, Purdue University, 1932

Journalists:

The following list of high achievers in both print and non-print media indicates that English majors have played a broad mix of leadership roles in journalism for a very long time.

Natalie Angier (*New York Times* Science Writer; 1991 Pulitzer Prize for Beat Reporting)
    B.A. English (and Physics), Barnard College, 1978
Russell Baker (Essayist, Pulitzer Prizes 1979 for Commentary and 1983 for Biography)
    B.A. English, Johns Hopkins University, 1947
Dave Barry (Humorist, 1988 Pulitzer Prize for Commentary)
    B.A. English, Haverford College, 1969
Erma Bombeck (Humorist, *At Wit's End*)
    B.A. English, University of Dayton, 1949
Maureen Dowd (Columnist *New York Times*; 1999 Pulitzer Prize for Commentary)
    B.A. English, Catholic University, 1973
David Faber (CNBC Co-Anchor, 2006 Emmy for Outstanding Business Documentary)
    B.A. English, Tufts University, 1985
Meg Greenfield (Editorial Writer *Washington Post*; 1978 Pulitzer Prize)
    B.A. English, Smith College, 1952
Martin Greif (Managing Editor Time-Life Books, Co-founder Main Street Press)
    B.A. English, Hunter College, 1959; M.A. English, Princeton, 1961
Cathy Guisewite (Cartoonist, *Cathy*;1987 Emmy for Outstanding Animated Program)
    B.A. English, University of Michigan, 1972
Steve Liesman (Business Reporter, 1999 Pulitzer Prize for International Reporting)
    B.A. English, SUNY Buffalo, 1985
Anna Quindlen (Columnist *New York Times, Newsweek*; '92 Pulitzer for Commentary)
    B.A. English, Barnard College, 1974
Roger Rosenblatt (Essayist and Editor, *U.S. News and World Report*)
    Ph.D. English, Harvard University, 1968
Diane Sawyer (Co-Anchor, *Good Morning America*)
    B.A. English, Wellesley, 1967
Serge Schmemann (Editorial Page Editor, *International Herald Tribune*)
    B.A. English, Harvard University, 1967
Bob Woodward (Investigative journalist, co-author of *All the President's Men*)
    B.A. English, Yale University, 1965
Ken Wolf (Columnist and Entertainment News Producer, ABC)
    B.A. English, SUNY Buffalo, 1987
Tom Woolfe (*The Electric Kool-Aid Acid Test*; Developer of The New Journalism)
    B.A. English, Washington and Lee, 1951

Attorneys:

College English remains, as it has been for many years, one of the best possible preparations for a career in law, and one of the most common (along with Political Science, Economics, and History). One individual in particular, Kathleen Sullivan, was herself such a progressive student of literature at Cornell University that she completed not only what would be a major in English at any other college, but she also completed courses in French literature as well as multiple courses in classical literature in Latin. She was effectively a Comparative Literature major before the discipline of Comparative Literature existed at Cornell. She went on to become a renowned litigator and one of America's leading scholars of constitutional law. She is currently the Stanley Morrison Professor of Law at Stanford University.

The sheer number of successful American attorneys is so large that I have consciously limited myself to identifying the following handful to demonstrate not only that English-major attorneys can rise to high levels of leadership in their profession, but that they can also find creative ways of using their legal knowledge outside of the courtroom.

Angela Alioto (Legal News Pundit, San Francisco Politician)
    B.A. English, Lone Mountain College, 1971
William D. Andrews (Eli Goldston Professor of Law Emeritus, Harvard University)
    B.A. English, Amherst, 1952; LL.B. Harvard, 1955
Elizabeth Bartholet (Morris Wasserstein Public Interest Professor of Law, Harvard)
    B.A. English, Radcliffe College, 1962; J.D. Harvard, 1965
Drew S. Days (U.S. Solicitor General 1993-96; Professor Yale Law School)
    B.A. English, Hamilton College, 1963; LL.B Harvard 1966
Michael S. Greco (President of the American Bar Association 2006-2007)
    B.A. English, Princeton, 1965; J.D. Boston College, 1972
Laura Ingraham (Conservative Radio Host; Clerk for Justice Clarence Thomas)
    B.A. English, Dartmouth College, 1985; J.D. University of Virginia, 1991
Richard Posner (Judge, U.S. 7th Circuit; Professor, University of Chicago Law School)
    A.B. English, Yale University, 1959
Kathleen Sullivan (Professor of Law; Dean, Stanford Law School 1999-2004)
    B.A. College Scholar Program, Cornell University, 1976; J.D. Harvard, 1981
Scott Turrow (Best-selling Novelist; Partner in Sonnenschein, Nath, & Rosenthal)
    B.A. English Amherst, 1970; M.A.Writing, Stanford, 1974; J.D. Harvard, 1978

Doctors and Medical Researchers:

As Chapter 1 indicates, English majors have long worked in all areas of medicine. Though few nurses or medical doctors achieve celebrity status or even what we sometimes refer to as "notoriety," the following list of medical researchers and practitioners gives a snapshot of the breadth of work accomplished by English majors in medicine.

Frederick L. Greene (Chairman, General Surgery, Carolinas Medical Center)
> B.A. English, University of Virginia, 1966; M.D., Virginia, 1970

Lisa Toepp (Col. US Army, ret; Forensic Psychiatrist, State of Colorado)
> B.A. English, University of Illinois 1981; M.D., Loyola University, 1985

B.F. Skinner (Founder of Behavioral Psychology)
> B.A. English, Hamilton College, 1926

Roger Wolcott Sperry (1981 Nobel Prize for Physiology/Medicine)
> B.A. English, Oberlin College, 1935; Ph.D. Zoology, University of Chicago, 1941

Harold Varmus (1989 Nobel Prize; Director, National Institutes of Health 1993-2000)
> B.A. English, Amherst College, 1961; M.D. Columbia University, 1966

Government Figures:

As this book has argued in multiple chapters, the ability to look at hard issues from multiple perspectives is vital to success in government work. So, too, is the skill of civility, which allows adversaries to disagree without demonizing one another. Government work also requires that officials put forward a public voice and a public face in the spoken and written word. English majors, having developed those very skills throughout their college years, often move on to careers in all areas of government work.

Carol Browner (Head of the EPA, 1993-2001)
> B.A. English, University of Florida, 1977

Bob Casey Jr. (Pennsylvania Senator, 2007-present)
> B.A. English, Holy Cross, 1982

Gerry Connolly (Virginia Congressman, 2007-present)
> B.A. Literature, Maryknoll College, 1971

Mario Cuomo (Governor of New York 1983-94)
> B.A. English, St. John's University NY, 1953

Christopher Dodd (Connecticut Congressman 1974-80; Senator 1980-present)
> B.A. English, Providence College, 1966

William O. Douglas (Supreme Court Justice 1939-75)
> B.A. English, Whitman College, 1920

Donna Edwards (Florida Congresswoman 2006-present)
> B.A. English, Wake Forest University, 1980

Abe Fortas (Supreme Court Justice 1965-69)
> B.A. English, Southwestern University (now Rhodes College), 1930

Judd Gregg (New Hampshire Senator 1993-present, Governor 1989-93)
> B.A. English, Columbia University, 1969

Dan Lungren (CA Congressman 1978-88, 2004-present; CA Attorney General 1990-98)
> A.B. English, Notre Dame University, 1968

John Lynch (Governor of New Hampshire 2007-present; former CEO Knoll, Inc.)
> B.A. English, University of New Hampshire, 1974

Thurgood Marshall (Supreme Court Justice 1967-91)
    B.A. American Literature, Lincoln University PA, 1930
Eugene McCarthy (Minnesota Senator 1959-71 and Presidential Candidate 1968)
    B.A. English, St. John's University MN, 1935
Deval Patrick (Governor of Massachusetts 2007-present)
    B.A. English, Harvard University, 1978
Henry M. Paulson (Secretary of the Treasury 2006-2009)
    B.A. English, Dartmouth, 1968
Bill Posey (Florida Congressman 2008-present)
    B.A. English Literature, Washington and Jefferson College
William Proxmire (Wisconsin Senator 1957-89)
    B.A. English, Yale University, 1938
Donald Regan (U.S. Treasury Secretary 1981-85, White House Chief of Staff 1985-87)
    B.A. English, Harvard University, 1940
Sally Ride (Astronaut, the first American woman in space; Professor, UC San Diego)
    B.A. English, Stanford University, 1973
Ileana Ros-Lehtinen (Florida Congresswoman 1989-present)
    B.A. English, Florida International University, 1975
Jeanne Shaheen (Governor of New Hampshire 1996-2002, 2008 US Senator)
    B.A. English, Shippensburg University, 1969
Eric Shinesky (Secretary of Veteran's Affairs 2009-present; Army Chief of Staff 1998-2003)
    M.A. English, Duke University, 1976
Potter Stewart (Supreme Court Justice 1958-81)
    B.A. English, Yale University 1937
Clarence Thomas (Supreme Court Justice 1991-Present)
    B.A. English, Holy Cross, 1971
Pete Wilson (California Senator 1983-91, Governor of California 1991-99)
    B.A. English, Yale University, 1956

Business Leaders:

I place the English-major leaders in business and industry at the end, to emphasize once again that the skills of the English major are transferable and to demonstrate by the example of these business leaders' successes that English majors truly can do whatever they put their minds to. The positions listed reflect a mix of current and former business roles.

Tom Anderson (Co-Founder of My Space)
    B.A. Rhetoric and English, University of California at Berkeley, 1998
Charlie Baker (CEO Harvard Pilgrim Healthcare)
    B.A. English, Harvard University, 1979
Jill Barad (CEO Mattel)
    B.A. English, Queens College, 1973

Judson Bergman (CEO Envestnet Asset Management)
  B.A. Wheaton College (Illinois), 1979
Linda Bloodworth-Thomason (Creator/Writer *Designing Women*, *Evening Shade*)
  B.A. English, University of Missouri, 1969
Zoe Cruz (Co-President Morgan-Stanley)
  B.A. Literature, Harvard, 1977
Tim Donahue (President and CEO of Nextel)
  B.A. English, John Carroll University, 1971
Michael Eisner (CEO Disney)
  B.A. English, Denison University, 1964
Romney Evans (CEO True Jeans)
  B.A. English, University of Utah, 2003
A.D. Frazier, Jr. (CEO Danka Business Systems)
  B.A. English, University of North Carolina at Chapel-Hill
Kathryn Fuller (CEO World Wildlife Fund)
  B.A. English, Brown University, 1968
Donald Graham (CEO Washington Post Company)
  B.A. English History and Literature, Harvard University, 1966
Robert Greifeld (President and CEO of NASDAQ)
  B.A. English, Iona College, 1979
Archibald Gwathmey (CEO Bunge Global Agribusiness)
  B.A. Classics and English, Harvard
Jerry Johnson (Founder, Chairman, and CEO of Mercantile Bank, Michigan)
  B.A. English, Hanover College, 1969
Andrea Jung (CEO Avon)
  B.A. English, Princeton, 1979
Sherry Lansing (President, Paramount Motion Pictures Group)
  B.S. English, Northwestern University, 1966
Aylwin Lewis (President and CEO Potbelly Sandwich Works, Sears Holdings Corp.)
  B.A. English, University of Houston, 1976
Michael Lynne (Co-Chairman and Co-CEO New-Line Cinema)
  B.A. English, Brooklyn College, 1961
Judith Ann McGrath (CEO MTV Networks Group)
  B.A. English, Cedar Crest College, 1974
Anne Mulcahy (CEO and Chairman of the Board, Xerox)
  B.A. English, Marymount College, 1974
John Muller (Chairman, General Counsel and Secretary, Paypal)
  B.A. English, University of Virginia, 1983
Robert S. Morrison (CEO Kraft, Quaker Oats, 3M)
  B.A. English, Holy Cross, 1963
Richard E. Posey (President and CEO of Moen Inc.)
  B.A. English, University of Southern California

Donald Regan (CEO Merril Lynch)
    B.A. English, Harvard University, 1940
Janet L. Robinson (President and CEO, The New York Times Company)
    B.A. English, Salve Regina College, 1972
James F. Rothenberg (President Capital Research and Management)
    B.A. English, Harvard, 1968
Herb Scannell (President, Nickelodeon Networks, MTV Networks Group President)
    B.A. English, Boston College, 1979
Joseph Sergeant (President and CEO, Guardian Life)
    B.A. English, Fairfield University, 1959
Brandon Tartikoff (President, Paramount; Chairman, New World Entertainment)
    B.A. English, Yale University, 1970
Jeri Taylor (TV Producer/Director *Star Trek: Voyager* and *The Next Generation*)
    B.A. English, Indiana Univ., 1959; M.A. English, Cal State University Northridge
Robert Thornton (Vice-President and General Counsel, Caterpillar Inc.)
    B.A. English, Georgetown University, 1950
Grant Tinker (Chairman and CEO of NBC)
    B.A. English, Dartmouth College, 1949
Seth Waugh (CEO Deutsche Bank Americas)
    B.A. English, Amherst College, 1980

Returning, then, to Thomas Gray's immortal point about success, I have laid out here only a few of those English majors who have gained national and international prominence in their chosen fields. At every lower stage of leadership, at every other stage of responsibility in all walks of life, you will also find English majors. They work as secret service agents, fire fighters, nurse practitioners, brewmasters, drug-store managers, ministers and nuns, public-transportation administrators, and landscapers. Whatever they do for a living, they do it with a foundation in the humanistic tradition, in which their ability to communicate with others is premised in their powers of imagination, in their ability to know what their needs are and to meet those needs with both words and actions.

Every person in this "Hall of Fame" is a thoughtful reader, deeply attuned to the human condition and to the creative arts. Everyone here approached his or her career with an uncanny ability to make things better in their place of business by what they thought, by what they said, and by what they wrote. When these people began their careers, they were simply English graduates in their twenties looking at a highly uncertain future, with no sure knowledge of how far their gifts would take them. All English majors have that same calling to take their English skills set out into the world when they graduate and to change things for the better in some way. There can be no contribution too humble in its origins, and no career path where they are not both needed and welcome.

CPSIA information can be obtained
at www.ICGtesting.com
Printed in the USA
FFOW01n1328300817
39397FF